The Overloving Parent

The Overloving Parent

Beverly Browning Runyon

Taylor Publishing Company
Dallas, Texas

Published by Taylor Publishing Company
            1550 West Mockingbird Lane
            Dallas, Texas 75235

Designed by Gary Hespenheide
Chapter art by Dennis Hill

Library of Congress Cataloging-in-Publication Data

Runyon, Beverly Browning.
    The overloving parent : making love work for you and your child /
Beverly Browning Runyon.
        p.   cm.
    ISBN 0-87833-803-9
    1. Parent and child—United States.   2. Parenting—United States.
3. Love—United States.   I. Title
HQ755.85.R86   1992
649′.1—dc20   92-15071
                                                                  CIP

Printed in the United States of America
10   9   8   7   6   5   4   3   2   1

*To Ashley, John Holt, and Chelsea, who
taught me the most about unconditional love
and making dreams come true.*

Acknowledgments

I want to thank the following people: my loving and support-ive husband, Bill, who I cherish; my wonderful parents, who built my self-esteem and taught me how to be a parent; Beth, Billy, and John, who welcomed me with acceptance and open arms; my dearest friends, Anita, Carolyn, D'Ann, Nancy, Courtney, Marty, Nelda, Carole, Ann, Joan, Judie, Susie, Pam, Martha, Kay, and Jo Marie, who encouraged and cheered; Lynn Searcy, for whom this thank you is too late, for telling me I could do anything I set a goal to do; the Fort Worth Literary Guild, who stimulate and challenge me intellectually; and finally, Dr. Karen Hayter, the COPE staff, and the many COPE viewers who suggested I write a book.

Finally, I want to thank the many parents I have worked with and advised who want love to work for themselves and their children.

CONTENTS

Appendices

The Overloving Parent

Introduction

This book is about parents who sincerely love their children. It is about parents who express their love to their children in many different kinds of ways—some of their expressions of love work and some fail. Loving parents may win or lose battles or they may win or lose relationships with their children. The outcome doesn't depend on how much they love their children or on the quality or quantity of their love. Their parenting success depends on *how* they love their children—on the ways they choose to express their love.

As a family consultant and parenting expert, I have advised many parents during the past fifteen years. Many of them were parents who loved their children in ways that were counterproductive or even destructive. Here I will share their stories with you in hopes that their experiences and my advice to them will help you identify and change the patterns that prevent you from becoming the most effective parent you can be.

All of the parents profiled in the following pages have the same problem, although their circumstances are greatly varied: They truly love their children and their love is not working the way they had wanted it to work. They all had the best intentions, hopes, and dreams for their children. Upon embracing parenthood, not one of them expected to feel as helpless, scared, frustrated, angry, or disappointed as they did when they called me and asked for help.

At first the parenting calls for help or advice came to me at the Parenting Guidance Center, a nonprofit, United Way Agency whose goals are to prevent child abuse and neglect and to promote positive parenting practices. The center is located in Fort Worth, Texas. I served briefly as founding president of the board of directors and subsequently began my professional career as a parenting advisor and consultant there.

Eight years ago I began appearing weekly on the news of the Dallas/Fort Worth NBC affiliate, KXAS-TV, delivering parenting advice and child-development information. I was impressed with the love and concern I heard in the voices and words of the parents who called in. Their stories of child-rearing practices varied, while their love and good intentions remained constant. But their love had not worked the way they had believed love should work.

In addition to my lectures and workshops through the Parenting Guidance Center and my weekly appearances on KXAS-TV as the parenting advisor for Dallas and Fort Worth, I was fortunate to be a regularly scheduled guest on Cope, the nationally syndicated, live call-in television show, which is seen in hundreds of cities around North America through the ACTS Network. Cope helps countless people by answering their questions about every mental health issue, from depression and abuse to addictions and parenting. I am honored to participate in Cope's "parenting Tuesdays," the day of the week dedicated to fielding questions about parenting and child development.

I have learned so much, not only from Cope's professional staff, which is headed by Dr. Karen Hayter, but also from the concerned parents who called Cope's toll-free telephone line for parenting advice. I have Dr. Hayter and the parents I've counseled to thank for giving me the impetus and encouragement to write this book. Without their support I might not have ever presented you with the following work.

Much of my research comes from reviewing footage from my appearances on Cope. As I reviewed the material from past programs, two of my beliefs about contemporary parenting were confirmed: Parents today face more difficulties in rearing their children than parents of past generations and that simply loving your children does not guarantee your success as a parent. Time and time again, parents have told me that they acted the way they did because they loved their children. Whether they had been too strict or too lenient, had given too little or too much, had been too rigid or too acquiescent, or had controlled too much or too little, these parents were trying to do their best, based on how their parents had reared them and on what they thought was in the best interest of their children.

I extended my heart and words of advice to these parents and now I offer them to all parents who seek help, answers, reassurance, encouragement, and knowledge because they want to be the best parents they can be.

My goal is to share what I have learned at the Parenting Guidance Center, at KXAS-TV, on Cope, from raising three children and being involved with three stepchildren, and from every parent I have worked with or known. I have selected true stories of parents who may have loved too much, or loved their children in ways that either did not work or did not even feel like love to their children. I will also provide examples of parents who reared their children in loving ways that were very successful. My purpose is to give practical advice, not easy solutions, for the parenting problems that I believe to be most common. The universal concerns of parents, which I have heard repeated in a variety of ways, and my insights and answers to those concerns make up this book.

This is not just a parenting book. It is a book about love, and more specifically, it is about when and why love doesn't always work. During my experience as a parenting consultant, I have identified four types of parents whose love has been misguided. Together we will explore the aspirations and responses of these four parental types and learn why they were unsuccessful in loving their children in positive ways. Each chapter will be followed by questions to help you determine which destructive pattern you may be using, and you will learn ways to change your own pattern of parenting. All parents want their love to work, so I will conclude with tips on loving discipline that will reinforce successful parenting techniques. I invite you now to survey the panorama of parenting love with me.

The Parent Trap:
Unrealistic Hopes and Dreams

Most adolescents hope to be married and have children some day. Adolescents look around at friends, at those more and less popular, and at other families, and begin to think about what they want from their future. Very few adolescents are satisfied enough with their lives that they would run their dream families the same way their parents have. Even the most successful and happy teens intend to do some things better than their parents did. Those who live in abusive or neglectful homes promise themselves that they will do almost everything better. And we all pray that they will.

In reality, however, very few of us make drastic changes in the way we parent from the way we were parented. But it is never too late to change our parenting techniques. Parenting is a learned skill that can always be improved by observing other parents, reading parenting books, and attending parenting classes, workshops, and programs.

Do you remember the Broadway musical *Carousel*, in which actor Gordon MacRae discovers that his co-star

Shirley Jones is pregnant with his child? He begins to fantasize about what his son will be like. In the middle of his wishful song, "My Boy Bill," it occurs to him that his son might be a daughter, and the song merely changes into a new fantasy about a daughter. His son is going to be as tall and as strong as an oak tree. His daughter is going to be the most beautiful girl that ever lived. We may not burst into song about how wonderful our children are going to be and how we will be terrific parents, but expectant parents do have fantastic dreams about parenthood.

Having dreams and aspirations for our children is normal and healthy. The problem develops when our children do not want to live our dreams or are not capable of making our fantasies come to life. If you add a parent who was reared in a dysfunctional family to the scenario, the product may be parents who love their children too much—parents who cling to a dream and try desperately, in excessive ways, to make that dream come true. These parents may be incapable of unconditionally loving their children. Later we will explore unconditional love more deeply, but for now think of unconditional love as one that is not dependent on a child's success, attractiveness, or accomplishments.

Parents who love too much fall into at least one of four different parenting styles used to control their children: those who **give and give in**, those who **push and punish**, those who **criticize and control**, and those who **defend and deny**. Their goal is to make their children into the children of their hopes and dreams.

But what each of these four types of parents have in common is that their love does not feel like love to their children—and it will *never* feel like love. Intellectually their children may know that their parents act out of love, but emotionally they do not feel truly loved. Simply enough, too much love does not work like healthy love in building self-esteem and independence, and in creating responsible and happy children.

Looking at the Parent Profiles

The following descriptions introduce the four types of parents who love in unproductive ways and may give you an idea of which category best describes you. Avoid the tendency to deny identification with one of the types because you do not fit all the characteristics. The following summaries give a brief overview of the chapters for each type, which provide more in-depth portraits and explanations and a Trait Inventory Test to help you identify your parenting style.

Remember most of these types of parents believe they are experiencing success with their techniques. Some parents have realized that their love and actions are not working and may want to make a few changes. Others may be desperate for help, but do not know where to begin to change or how to change.

No one will have all of the characteristics associated with any one of the four types of overloving parents because every parent is unique. However, if you realize you have some similarities, be sure to read the involved descriptions and analyses of each type of parent in the following chapters. Try to recognize which type of parent you share more similarities with and study the corresponding chapter carefully. Remember there are many degrees of loving too much. You may be looking for just a tendency or an inclination that is prevalent among one of the four types of parents. Do not be too hasty to label a case study as extreme or a set of descriptions as having no relevance to you. Look for the lessons to be learned.

Parents Who Give and Give In

Recently on the Cope television program the sweetest sounding mother, named Ginger, called about her eight-year-old daughter:

"I don't know what to do about my little girl," she began. "She won't take no for an answer. I have two younger children and by the end of the day I'm tired. My eight-year-old keeps asking or pleading for whatever I have said no to. My husband is trying to relax and looks at me like I have got to make her be quiet. I want everybody to be happy so I give in. What can I do? I don't want to give in, but she wears me down and it just seems easier."

My conversation and advice to Ginger will be discussed later, but I hope you will focus on the words that told me that this is a mother who gives and gives in, not only to her daughter but probably to most of the significant people in her life. The first sign is that Ginger's eight-year-old won't take no for an answer. The second red flag is Ginger's justification for giving in: "she keeps asking or pleading." The next clue is that Ginger's husband expects her to make the problem go away. Ginger's sole responsibility and goal, to make everyone happy, is draining her energy and causing her to be an ineffective parent.

Ginger loves her child more than she loves herself. Like other parents who give and give in, Ginger always strives to please others before she pleases herself. Parents who give and give in are great at helping others. They are good at consoling, listening, serving, sacrificing, and supporting. But overly giving parents are not very good at setting limits or boundaries, enforcing rules, sticking to a schedule, being assertive or decisive, or taking control.

The problem with giving and giving in too much is that this form of loving can backfire on the parent. The various consequences for the parent and the child will be discussed later, but in extreme cases the children resent their loving parents, have an extremely low self-esteem, and grow up to be narcissistic and irresponsible. Both parent and child may then suffer from depression and stress-related illnesses.

Parents Who Push and Punish

Pat, a parent who pushes and punishes, called me for advice and possibly approval. A classic example of this type of parent, he began with:

"My five-year-old son is a very strong-willed child. He is so difficult. He is always finding something to get into, which just infuriates me. He has so much energy and can't sit still. It is like he is trying to make me mad. I punish him all the time, but it doesn't seem to make him any better. I'm determined to shape him up before he starts school so he won't be a problem there like he is here. He knows I'm doing this for his own good. He will never amount to anything, if he doesn't learn to mind. I need some new ideas on making him respect my authority."

In questioning Pat, I developed a much clearer picture of what he was like—a parent who punishes more than he pushes his child. (I suspect if his son were more compliant and not as "strong willed," Pat would have had more opportunity to be a pushing parent.) On a surface level, several important observations about this kind of parent can be made from examining Pat's opening statement.

Pat's exasperation with his son's typical five-year-old behavior is common in parents who push and punish as their way of expressing love. The parent who excessively punishes frequently views age-appropriate behavior as an attempt on the child's part to aggravate them, as Pat describes.

Moreover, Pat's openness about constantly punishing his son and his sincere belief that the punishment—no matter how frequent or how severe—is for his son's own good characterizes Pat as a parent who truly loves his child, but who expresses his love by pushing and punishing too much.

In general, parents who push and punish excessively have high expectations and are good at setting limits and enforcing them, taking action, and coaching and striving for perfection. This type of parent is not sympathetic or sensitive, lacks patience and tolerance, and wants to see results and success. Unfortunately, the result can be the physical and emotional abuse of his child. The consequence for the child can be severe emotional and sociopathic problems, which ultimately affects our society as well. Our prisons are full of adults who were abused as children.

In less serious cases, parents who push and punish just a little too much, can expect to have children who become overachievers who distance themselves from their parents as soon as possible, or underachievers who stop trying to please their demanding parents, also distancing themselves from their parents as soon as possible. In either scenario, this type of loving parent loses.

Parents Who Criticize and Control

I was fielding parents' questions on the Cope television program with the host and producer of the program, Dr. Karen Hayter, when Carol called, requesting advice.

"I need some advice about my eleven-year-old son, Jordan," Carol announced. "He is an exceptionally bright boy who has always excelled in school until the end of last year and all this year."

Dr. Hayter wisely asked Carol if she could be more specific with her problem.

Carol responded, "I'll try to be specific, but first I need to share some general information about Jordan. When he was just a toddler, we knew he was a gifted child. By four he was reading and at five in kindergarten his teacher also recognized his high IQ. He has always been in accelerated or honors classes and has always performed at the top of his class. The last year he has been a real disappointment. Not only is he not performing at his potential, but he is not trying. He is not a discipline problem, but we are so dissatisfied with his attitude.

"I have very strict rules, such as no television on school days and nights. He is to be in bed on school nights by 8:30. And there is no play until his homework is done. He gets a healthy snack after school, and then I tell him to start his homework. This has always worked well until he turned ten. He has lied to me about his homework being done because I have recently received a note from his teacher saying his homework has not been completed. His grades have dropped from straight A's to mostly C's and a couple of B's.

"Now his teacher is talking about taking him out of the honors classes and putting him back in the regular classes. We don't know what we would do if this happened to us. We know he is so capable if he would just listen to us and do what we say. He has changed and I am determined to get this situation under control. I have tried grounding, taking away his computer games, and putting him to bed earlier.

"I suspect that his change in attitude has something to do with his friends at school. I know it is not his neighborhood friends because I made sure of that several years ago when he began to play with some neighborhood boys whose parents were always at work and never supervised their children. I only allowed him to make friends with the children in our block whose parents are conscientious like we are.

"Now to my question: How can I make Jordan take his schoolwork more seriously and not be like so many kids today who never work hard or learn to make some sacrifices now so they can be prepared for the future?"

Carol is obviously a parent who loves her son very much, but her love is unproductive because her style of parenting is criticizing and controlling.

It is not difficult to spot the criticizing and controlling clues. Amazingly, however, parents like Carol do not realize they sound that way. Looking at others in a critical way and believing that it is their role to advise others is so much a part of their way of thinking that it has become more than their role, it has become their mission.

Someone like Carol can see so clearly how something should be done that she is amazed that the rest of the world does not see it. For example, when other parents do not appear to be as conscientious as Carol believes she is, Carol dismisses them as irresponsible. She does not make an effort to get to know these parents and to negotiate a way for her son to play with their children. Her decision is unilateral: Her child will not play with those children.

Carol's efforts at controlling her son most likely started before his birth. Like most parents, she dreamed about what her child would be like and what a good parent she would be. But unlike most parents, Carol thought it was within her power to make her son into the person of her dreams. When he was born, he cooperated with her dream. He most likely surpassed all the pediatric tests of child development by crawling, walking, and talking much sooner than the average child. Carol's dream was coming true. Then her hours of reading to him and showing him alphabet flash cards began to pay off and he was reading by age four.

It does not take much encouragement for a controlling parent to increase her amount of control. As her son gets older and more capable, instead of letting go or encouraging some independence, Carol tightens her hold. She becomes more involved in her son's daily life, thereby securing his and her future as the best mother-son team of all time—and her dream lives on.

I have briefly addressed Carol's critical attitude toward others who are different from herself and her controlling style with her son. But before I describe the other traits that criticizing and controlling parents like Carol have in common, I want to draw attention to her critical posture toward her son.

Carol probably did not have critical feelings about her son in earlier years. He was always the first and the brightest in her eyes and probably to others as well. Carol's success in having a child that lived up to her dreams allowed her to focus her criticisms on other parents who were seemingly less successful with their children. Most likely, Carol assumed that if they parented more like her, their children would be more like her son. However, when Carol's controlling parenting techniques stopped paying dividends, her critical eye turned not toward herself, but toward her son. When Carol describes her son as a "disappointment" and says he has the wrong attitude, she is choosing to assess his character critically, instead of looking for the cause of his change in behavior. Carol wants results and facts, not feelings or expressions of needs.

Carol and other parents who express their love primarily through criticizing and controlling are very self-disciplined and like others to be that way too. However, if their children are not inclined to be self-disciplined, these parents will consistently work to correct this weakness. They usually succeed because criticizing and controlling parents can be relentless in their attempts to satisfy their goals for their children. They also tend to be perfectionists, organized, predictable, and very neat. Criticizing and controlling parents are not good at being flexible and open listeners, who easily tend to feelings or give approval.

The consequences for the child of a criticizing and controlling parent generally range from having low self-esteem, lacking confidence, and feeling inadequate, to being obsessive, compulsive, or lonely, and choosing a life of unattainable goals that reproduce their childhood feelings of never being quite good enough. As adults, the children of controlling parents live with dangerously high levels of self-induced stress and view the world in an adversarial way.

Children of parents who are mildly critical and controlling are usually very organized, detail-oriented, punctual, and neat. They may have trouble making decisions because there is never the perfect choice or because they are accustomed to having their parents make decisions for them. More specifically, they may also overindulge in fun during their first year in college when they are away from the eyes and ears of their controlling parents. Excessive eating, drinking, partying, and skipping class are not unusual habits for freshmen who are enjoying new freedom from controlling parents.

Parents Who Defend and Deny

Most of the parents who seek my parenting advice have children who are infants, toddlers, elementary school age or teenagers. As a result, Donna presented me with a less familiar case when she explained her situation:

"I am a single parent of a twenty-eight-year-old daughter, who is married, and my son, Timmy, who lives with me. I want some advice about Timmy. My son is twenty-five, and he won't respect my rules. You see I'm tired of Timmy coming in at all hours, leaving his mess of beer cans, messy ashtrays, food left out in the kitchen overnight, and his clothes and junk all over the house. I know when he finds a job, he'll be gone more and he'll get to bed at a decent hour because he'll be getting up for work each morning, but I don't know when that will be. It seems like all my nagging and complaining doesn't seem to change him.

"He's a good boy who has had a run of bad luck all his life. He was such a cute little boy and a real charmer. His teachers just adored him until middle school and that's when the girls began to adore him. His dad and I divorced when he was seven, and I married again when he was twelve. Timmy and his step-dad never got along. His step-dad was always on him about something. I could not stay married to someone my Timmy did not like.

"Timmy would have made a star football player in college and probably would have gotten a scholarship, but his coach just had it in for him. He graduated from high school but he decided to put off college for a year or so. Timmy has not been able to find a job he likes and he has lost interest in college. I think he has fallen in with a bad crowd of friends. All they do is stay out late drinking and chasing girls.

"Do you think I am wrong to ask Timmy to do more around the house and respect my rules? I know this is hard on him to keep looking for a job. It is real discouraging to get turned down all the time. But I'm tired of the way he talks to me and doesn't do the few things I ask him to do. What should I do?"

Donna's love for her son is so misdirected that it compels her to defend him and systematically deny his problems. Timmy probably doesn't even think he has problems because his mom has always handled them or assumed them as her own. Some days all of us wish we had a Donna to take care of us and make our responsibilities and problems go away. However, after a short time of relinquishing our responsibilities and problems to someone like Donna, we would realize that we also gave up our independence, pride, and self-esteem. Like Timmy we would begin to feel worthless, and selfish, as if the rest of the world owes us something. We would also become terrific manipulators with prepared excuses for our failures. Our excuses would consistently blame others and suggest our own bad luck.

Donna probably began her parenting by making excuses for Timmy. She probably overlooked his minor misbehavior at first and then started rescuing him from his more significant mistakes. By the time Timmy was school age, he was skilled beyond his years at manipulating adults, particularly women. Thus many of his teachers probably overlooked his shortcomings and focused on his potential. More than likely Donna began to interfere on his behalf even more, by providing excuses, such as she threw away his homework by mistake, to make up for his irresponsible behavior. Probably few teachers challenged Donna's efforts to keep Timmy from staying after school for detention or from failing.

I suspect that elementary school for Timmy was relatively free of consequences, or so it seemed. As with the other forms of loving too much, the consequences of being reared by a parent who defends and denies do not become apparent immediately. It had taken Donna twenty-five years to ask for help. Even now she needed reassurance that she was not asking too much of Timmy to obey a few house rules and treat her with respect.

Predictably, it was more difficult for Timmy to manipulate his teachers in middle school, but with Donna working for him he escaped with only a few bad grades and brief visits to the principal's office. Now he had added several more adults to his defensive lineup—the coaches in his life. His athletic potential was a coach's dream. And since he wore the sympathetic labels, "product of a divorce" and "raised by a single mother," his coaches enjoyed acting as a father figure to him. In short, they were also quick to make excuses for him because he seemed to deserve the protection and because they thought they could "turn him around."

It sounds as if high school had one redeeming factor—girls. Where his mother and his coaches left off, the girls in Timmy's life stepped in. Like the other enablers Timmy attracted, his girlfriends also defended Timmy and made excuses for his behavior. Presumably Donna was not threatened by his girlfriends. She was tired and knew her limitations, and she must have adored anyone who adored her son. By now Donna had advanced from just defending Timmy to denying that he was troubled in many ways. When parents move into denial, they have reached the advanced stage of a destructive love.

Parents like Donna, who express their love by defending and denying, are too patient. Unaware of reality, they evade their children's problems. They also relinquish control over their own lives when they assume responsibility for their children's actions. Their children's feelings and needs always supersede their own. Parents like Donna are codependent on their children and enablers of their children's misbehavior and mistakes. For Timmy and other children who have been raised by parents who depend on their children to need them, the consequences can be frightening. Timmy views the world as "unfair," he considers failures to be "bad luck," and contends that anyone he cannot manipulate has it in for him.

Usually people like Timmy find replacements for their exhausted parents to forgive and forget their mistakes and to cover up the evidence of their misdeeds. The replacements are people who are sure they can change the Timmys of this world. These replacements act like surrogate parents who at first thrive on helping, rescuing and just "being there" for Timmy. They enable Timmy to continue to be irresponsible and unaccountable for his actions—until their own energy runs out.

Enablers seem to come out of the woodwork whenever Timmy wears out the current rescuer. Timmy will appear to be getting his act together for awhile, and the enabling guardian will feel like he or she has made a difference in Timmy's life. Then the cycle of so-called "bad luck" begins again. This will not curb the rescuing efforts of the new enabler, whose efforts to support and encourage will only accelerate for a while until she or he becomes too exhausted and discouraged.

In extreme cases, and in all too many cases, children of parents who defend and deny become adults who cannot function within societal constraints. Prisons are full of Timmys.

Parents Who Choose to Change

Once overloving parents have identified their problem, they begin to realize the consequences of their well-meaning but damaging love. Many of these parents become aware of their problem in the early stages of excessive love and learn new ways of parenting. They develop healthier ways of expressing their love through proven parenting techniques. Even so, it may be many months from the time when parents begin to question the success of their parenting techniques to the time when they contemplate trying something different. All the while their children may be moving deeper into dysfunctional patterns of behavior.

The time between realization and action may be so long because many parents want their children to change, and they do not realize that their children's chances of changing depend on their own ability to change first. The process of helping children improve their behavior must begin with the parents taking the first step by trying a new way to express their love.

But before parents are capable of taking the first step in changing their relationships with their children, parents must realize the necessity for those changes. Thus the first step is becoming aware that a negative pattern is developing. For some parents it is even more difficult to foresee the consequences their parenting style will have on their children's development. For other parents the consequences are already becoming evident and their fears are becoming a reality. They are desperate for help.

By reading about the many different parents who didn't see the need to change their parenting styles until their children's problems became too difficult to handle, I hope you will learn to recognize similar tendencies in yourself. After identifying your own dysfunctional pattern, the second step is understanding the potential consequences of your style of parenting. Some of the consequences are severe and even life-threatening. Making changes in your parenting style before your child reaches adolescence will prevent unnecessary problems from occurring. The third step is having the desire to change. Desire is induced by recognizing a problem or tendency, believing the possible negative consequences, and assuming the responsibility to change yourself first.

Change truly begins with your desire to be a better parent. My goal is to ignite that desire and show you why it is so important to change. The following stories are intended to alert you to destructive parenting patterns, to demonstrate their possible consequences, and to inspire you to make the necessary changes. And ultimately, my goal is to teach you new parenting skills that will help you be the best parent you can be.

Parents Who Give and Give In

When they were younger, the parents who give too much and the parents who give in probably fantasized about having a dream child who would love them completely. By giving, I mean giving gifts or money, making personal sacrifices of time and talent, and serving—doing for children what they are quite capable of doing for themselves. Of course all parents want their children to love them, but these parents' need for love is different. Their need for love comes from having low self-esteem. As a result, these parents not only need to be loved, they also need to be liked. But being a responsible parent does not always mean being liked by our children. Often our children are very angry about decisions we make or rules we set. The type of parents who give too much or give in are extremely uncomfortable with their children's anger, especially if it is directed at them.

Grace: Living with the Consequences of Giving Too Much

It is time to hear from a parent who gives too much. Grace called about her seventeen-year-old daughter, Ann. She began our discussion by saying, "I am worried about my daughter. She has been the light of my life until she was about eleven. Now she is moody, difficult, and demanding."

At first I thought I should explain the developmental stages of an adolescent and the typical behavior of that age. However, I was surprised that Grace would wait until Ann was seventeen to seek advice about her attitude. Usually moodiness is characteristic of early adolescence and mellows out by seventeen, which is considered the middle of adolescence. As I listened to more of Grace's story, I realized she was describing more than the typical adolescent problems.

"I know I have probably spoiled her," Grace continued, "but she is such a pretty girl that it has always been fun to buy her clothes. Ann is also not as easy to get along with as her two older brothers. Whenever Ann is in a bad mood, the quickest way to perk her up is to buy her a little surprise. Ann always seemed to get her self-confidence from the way she looked. Even in elementary school the boys noticed her. Ann had a few girlfriends too.

"Ann, however, is not real good at keeping friends. I think her moodiness runs her friends off, but it does not seem to run the boys off. She is popular but not a good student. She has never been what I would call a happy child.

"I learned to stay away from her in the mornings. Ann is just not a morning person. After school she is tired and irritable. The teachers always said Ann was perfect in class. She always made good grades in citizenship. It was just at home that she would lose her temper.

"Ann has always liked to shop. She loves clothes and makeup like most girls. She simply had more than most of her friends. I'm sure I have let her have too much. There is always some special occasion or party, and she never wants to wear the same thing. She is so excited and acts so happy when she is dressed up and ready to go out."

At this point in the conversation I interrupted Grace to ask, "Does Ann ever help pay for her clothes?"

"Actually Ann has paid for some of her clothes. She had a job last summer and used her earnings to add to her wardrobe. But that did not decrease the amount of money I spent on her. She just bought more. It is hard for Ann to have a job after school because she has so much homework. It is difficult for her to keep up with her schoolwork.

"My problem with Ann now is not a big one, I am just worried that she is not a happy girl when she has so many reasons to be happy. We still don't get along well. I never seem to please her except when we shop, and even that usually turns into a fight because she always wants more than I am willing to buy. Sometimes I feel like I am a failure as her mother."

"I do not agree that your problem with Ann is a small one," I began, "any time a parent tells me that they feel like a failure I consider the problem to be serious."

As a parent who typically shows her love by giving too much, Grace turned the conversation away from Ann's behavioral problems, saying, "Well, she is not on drugs.

She hasn't run away. She is planning on going to college. I think I have just spoiled her."

I tried to reassure Grace. "By taking your problem seriously, I mean that I believe you feel like a failure even though Ann is not in a life-threatening situation. I feel sure she will go to college. She probably appears to be doing great to outsiders. But I also trust your instincts that Ann is an unhappy girl. I recognize your efforts to please her and understand that you feel helpless when it comes to handling her moodiness. I also think you are a very loving mother. Perhaps you have loved Ann too much. Let me explain what I mean by loving too much."

When some types of parents love too much, they are often reluctant to set limits and boundaries. The loving parent may fear that saying no will jeopardize the child's love for him or her. Some loving parents hope that if they make sacrifices for their children and give them gifts, their children will feel warmth, love, and gratitude toward them. These parents want more than a thank you for what they give—they want love in return.

I asked Grace if she had a very giving parent that she loved dearly as a child. I also asked her if she had been a very obedient, grateful daughter. Grace confirmed that this was indeed the case. "The way your mother parented you has not worked with Ann, at least it has not produced the same results," I told her. "Perhaps your mother was very loving but also firmer with you," I added. Ann also agreed with this.

I began to explain to Grace how her parenting had influenced Ann's behavior by telling her, "At first small surprises would bring joy to Ann's sad face. By catering to her you could win her approval. You were generous to a fault because your generosity was rooted in your need for acceptance. Ann's price for approval and acceptance grew bigger as she grew bigger.

"Your self-esteem is dependent on other people's love for you, particularly Ann. Ann's self-esteem is dependent on how she looks and what she has. Shopping for Ann gives her a high and wins you a few moments of her approval and acceptance. As you have learned, those moments are expensive and fleeting.

"What will Ann do when you are not around? Do you think she will be able to support herself in the lifestyle she has grown accustomed to? Do you think she will find someone who will continue to give at the level you have prepared her to expect?"

Grace responded, "I have thought about all those things, and I am very concerned about Ann's future. I have heard of parents who continue to support their children after college. I don't believe in that, but I can see how it happens. You just don't wake up one day and start saying no."

I cautioned, "Changing the way you parent is not easy and it certainly does not happen over night. But it is possible to change, especially when you understand the consequences of your parenting pattern.

"Your excessive need for Ann's approval and your fear of losing her love have left you vulnerable to her moods and her insensitive words. In contrast to your sensitivity, Ann has become a demanding, self-centered teenager. Instead of taking a drug to numb negative feelings, Ann shops. You have become the enabler of her addiction—shopping—and the dumping ground for her anger.

"It is never too late to change. However, you and Ann have well-established roles in this mother-daughter dance. I highly recommend that you both get individual counseling. I would recommend that Ann begin counseling by herself. She is not as motivated to change as you are. Ann is unhappy, but she also has a convenient arrangement with you as provider of her money and custodian of her moodiness. Individual counseling for you will be of utmost importance to adequately address the origin of your low self-esteem. You will also need professional support in the ongoing process of changing your parenting style. You have had at least seventeen years to develop and perfect your way of loving too much. Would you be willing to seek counseling for Ann and yourself?"

"Yes, I would," she replied, "but what if Ann will not go?"

I explained, "There are at least two ways of approaching Ann's resistance to counseling. First, you can tell her you are concerned about her unhappiness, which is the truth, and that you want her to talk to a counselor to help you be a better mother, which is also the truth. Or a more assertive way to approach Ann would be to tell her that you think both of you would benefit from going to individual counseling. If she does not choose to go, you need to prohibit all shopping sprees until she goes. She has a choice. I suspect the latter approach would be quite difficult for you, but it would certainly be a positive new behavior for you and an effective way of conveying to Ann that now you are in charge.

Ginger: Caught in the Cycle of Giving In

Closely aligned with the parent who gives too much is the parent who gives in too much. Do you remember Ginger, who was introduced in the first chapter, The Parent Trap?

Ginger was the young mother who called me for advice about how to handle her eight-year-old daughter, Hanna. Hanna could always "wear down" Ginger by pressuring her to change her mind when she had prohibited Hanna from doing or having something she wanted. At the end of a long stressful day of caring for Hanna and her two younger brothers, Ginger's resolve to stick to her decision would weaken. Under the critical eye of her husband, Ginger would give in to Hanna's unrelenting whine. As Ginger explained before, she gives in because she wants everyone to be happy.

I asked Ginger about her marriage because she had described her husband, Curt, as expecting her to keep Hanna quiet so he could relax after work. As I expected, Ginger defended him by saying, "Curt is a good husband and a hard worker. He just expects me to be a better wife and mother than I am. The house is not as tidy as he would like, dinner is not ready soon enough, and I obviously don't have control over Hanna."

"What does Curt do with Hanna? What kind of a parent do you think he is?" I asked.

"Well, Curt is very tired when he comes home so he doesn't really feel like doing anything with any of the children. Sometimes on weekends when he isn't playing golf, he will stay with the children while I run errands," Ginger answered, trying to rationalize his behavior.

It is fascinating to talk with someone like Ginger who is so reluctant to see faults in others, but who is so willing to heap blame upon herself. Ginger has very low self-esteem. Outwardly she may appear to be functioning relatively well, but inwardly she is crumbling.

Ginger can only feel good about herself when she can make everyone else happy, which is impossible for anyone to do. So Ginger is doomed to feel like a failure. She has also chosen to marry someone who will contribute to her low self-esteem. Having a critical personality, Curt will never express total approval of Ginger. Ginger will always feel inadequate. Ginger is probably recreating the inadequate feeling with which she is most familiar because she lives with a husband who acts like a negative and critical parent.

Ironically, Ginger's low self-esteem is contagious, and Hanna is the prime recipient of it. Whenever children are allowed to treat their parents disrespectfully, they may feel powerful at first, but then they will feel guilty about their behavior. Children may then resent their parents for allowing them to be rude. In anger, children may lash out at a parent who has not stood up to them. Or children may test the boundaries set by their parents to see if they will ever stick to their rules or limits.

Children do not tell their parents that they feel more secure with limits and boundaries, but they do. Instead, children of parents who give in too often will push, whine, beg, plead, nag, or persist until their parents weaken and give up. What they really want when they push and plead for yes, is a firm no. They need to know that their loving parent is stronger than they are. Being more powerful than their parents does not give them security. It is frightening for children who do not feel that their parents are in charge.

On the other hand, Ginger will probably be more assertive with her two younger children. Often parents who give and give in too much will only do this with one of their children. Hanna established her claim as the strong-willed child in the family. Hanna's younger brothers will resent the way Hanna talks to their mother and may compensate for Hanna's difficult behavior by being more cooperative and less demanding. Ginger will also have learned from her mistakes with Hanna, the first born, and will be more firm and consistent with her two younger children.

Ginger's friends will probably view Hanna as the problem because the other children are better behaved. Some will even suggest that Ginger should "just stand up" to her eight-year-old daughter. But I believe Ginger, not Hanna, is the problem. Unfortunately, Ginger's marriage is a significant factor in her inability to change her pattern of giving in as a way of coping. Ginger and Curt, or at least Ginger, should seek marriage counseling at this point because it would have a direct effect on their parenting skills and their relationship with Hanna. However, I would not be surprised if Ginger decided against seeing a marriage counselor because people with low self-esteem do not feel they deserve to get costly professional help. Instead she probably decided to try the other advice I gave her, which was to use consistent discipline techniques.

In order to convince Ginger that it was necessary to change her inconsistent discipline, I explained how allowing Hanna to nag her until she gave in would give Hanna low self-esteem. I knew that the only way to convince Ginger to change was to explain the consequences for Hanna. Because Ginger is a parent who loves too much, she is highly motivated by hearing what is best for her child. If I had tried to convince Ginger to change for herself, which is also a valid reason to change, Ginger would not have listened to my advice. Ginger will always put others before herself.

Before I discussed discipline with Ginger, I asked her how she disciplined Hanna. She replied, "I get mad and threaten to not let her go someplace or tell her she will have to go to her room. I really don't want to punish her. I want her to love me and to want to do what I ask her."

I explained to Ginger that children need to respect as well as love their parents—and it is difficult for children to love their parents if they do not respect them. Respect is earned by acting like a parent. Children need to know they are the children and that the parents are the adults. A clear generation gap creates an emotionally healthy parent-child relationship in which love can flourish.

This explanation seemed to make sense to Ginger, so I continued. "You and Hanna have your roles reversed. Hanna is acting like a demanding mother and you are acting like the inadequate child. What is essential for Hanna's self-esteem and for her future relationships, is that you seize your place as her mother. If you do not take charge now, what will you do when she is fourteen?"

Ginger admitted that she worried about the teenage years with Hanna, especially since she did not seem to be able to be firm with Hanna now. I told Ginger I believed she was capable of changing and Ginger said that she understood the importance of improving her parenting skills to help Hanna. I challenged Ginger, "Are you ready to learn how to be a more effective mother?" With a more determined voice Ginger replied, "Yes."

"First," I instructed, "you must make Hanna believe in you. This will not be easy because the new you is going to be different from the mother she is used to. She will not expect you to mean what you say. Hanna will still think she is in control of you, not that you are in charge of *her*. Hanna will try everything she can think of to bring back the mother she is familiar with. At first she will test your new resolve, then she'll acquiesce for a while, and then, when you least expect it, she will pull out all the stops to try to bring back the mother she knows best.

"Your job is to convince Hanna that the new you is here to stay. Even though your new approach to parenting will improve your self-esteem and Hanna's, she will resist the change. She will not realize for a while that having a mother who makes decisions and sticks to them will help her in future relationships and endeavors. Hanna will be learning to respect not only you, but other people too. She will be learning that rules are not made to be broken, but to be followed consistently.

"Hanna must be told what to expect. In a private meeting with Hanna, begin by apologizing to her. Tell her you have not been the kind of parent you want to be. Briefly share with Hanna your new understanding of the importance for the parents to be the parents and the kids to be the kids. Prepare her by telling her that a few important things are going to change. Tell her that when you say no in the future, you will mean it and stick to it. For a while you may be excessively rigid, until you learn to make decisions fairly.

"There will be one rule you will enforce every time it is broken: Hanna is not to argue, plead, nag, or whine in order to induce you to change your mind. Ask Hanna if she understands the rule and why you are making this very important rule. Do not allow her to argue with you about the rule because that is merely returning to your old pattern. She may ask for clarification or examples. Hanna does not have to like the rule, she just has to understand it.

"Now it is time to spell out the consequence of breaking the rule. Hanna will be sent to her room, the dining room, or any room you choose (preferably the same room and one that is uninteresting to a child). Hanna will stay in the designated room for eight minutes—one minute for each year of her age. If she chooses to break the rule again in the same day, she will go to the room for eight minutes plus five-to-eight minutes more. Each additional infraction of the rule will mean additional time in an uninteresting room for Hanna.

"Also explain to Hanna that you hope she chooses to obey the rule, but that you will understand that obedience will require a new way of behaving, a more respectful way of behaving. Tell her you know that she might not intentionally break the rule because you know she wants to be good; that when she disobeys you will assume that she just made a mistake by choosing not to act respectfully. But she will still have to experience the consequence. Hanna will learn to control her disrespectful behavior and you will have a consistent recourse if she lapses into unacceptable behavioral patterns.

"So when Hanna breaks the rule, and she will break the rule, remember that her goal is to see if she can make you revert to your old habit of giving in. Your goal is to convince Hanna that you are serious about being in charge and that you are capable of being her mother.

"The next time Hanna gives you an argument, speak calmly with confidence and say just a few words, such as, 'I see you have chosen to break the rule about being respectful. Go to the dining room for eight minutes.' When time is up say, 'Hanna, you may come out now. I'm sure you will do better next time.' It might also feel good to both of you if you give Hanna a hug. Children react more positively when they think their parents believe that they are good and can improve their behavior.

"At this point it might be helpful for both you and Hanna to know that it is okay for Hanna to be angry with you. What is not okay is the way you have allowed her to express her angry feelings. At first you will be very uncomfortable enforcing the rule instead of giving in to her anger. You may even be afraid that you are losing Hanna's love. Be reassured that Hanna will continue to love you— probably even more than she does now. Moreover, your consistent discipline will feel like love to her. Sometimes the most difficult way of expressing love for a giving person is to say no."

Ginger thought about what I had said and replied, "It sounds like a very different behavior for me, but it makes sense and it is the way I want to be. I think I can do it. I really want to be a stronger parent and I believe it is important to reclaim my role as mother."

I suggested that Ginger's husband may not be the safest person to share this plan with. Ginger agreed, explaining that he would be critical and she did not want the pressure of knowing he would be watching for failures. We agreed that Ginger might want to share her plans with a close, supportive friend or someone she could talk to about her fear of giving in to Hanna.

Last of all, I encouraged her again to seek counseling for herself, especially now that she acknowledged her low self-esteem and had expressed a desire to make some changes in her relationship with Hanna.

George: A Father Who Faced His Need to Give and Give In

Mothers are not the only parents who fall into the habit of giving and giving in too much. I was recently reminded of fathers who also parent this way when I saw a commercial for Volvo on television. In the commercial three children brag about their fathers. The first little boy says, "My daddy loves me so much he bought me a baseball bat and a video game." The next child brags how his father loves him more because his father buys him even more bats and video games. The third child tops them all by boasting, "My daddy loves me so much he bought a Volvo."

Fathers are commonly guilty of expressing their love by buying presents. Sometimes they feel guilty about being away from their children due to demanding work schedules. They believe their extravagant gifts are a way of making up for being absentee parents. George was not an absentee father, but he was a father who found himself in trouble because of his need to give and give in.

George was a very successful businessman who had grown up in a poor, single-parent home. He was bright, enthusiastic, and loved his son more than anyone or anything else. When we first talked, George's son, Tom, was twenty years old. George had taken Tom on fishing, hunting, and skiing trips since he was a little boy, and they had attended professional athletic events whenever possible. George always made time in his demanding work schedule to be the father he never had.

Tom always had the best hunting, fishing, and skiing equipment. He was entertained with the latest and best toys. Next came cameras, video games, and stereo equipment. Christmas and birthday gifts were inevitably extravagant. In short, George gave Tom everything he had wished for when he was a boy.

All went reasonably well until Tom got his driver's license and a terrific new sports car as a sixteenth birthday present from his dad. Shortly after, Tom's grades dropped and he lost interest in playing football. George accepted

Tom's excuses about his slipping grades. George was a little disappointed about the football resignation, but in some ways he was relieved because he worried about Tom being injured. George continued to have what he viewed as a rewarding and loving relationship with his son.

George was aware that Tom's friends changed, but he understood why Tom might not want to run around with his old football buddies. What worried George at first were Tom's speeding tickets. George knew it was hard for a teenage boy to resist driving a sports car above the speed limit, but he continually reminded Tom about the importance of wearing his seat belt and warned him about getting hurt. Tom applied his more than generous allowance toward attorney fees for representing him in traffic court.

George knew Tom drank. All boys that age did, or so George believed. George threatened to take Tom's car away if he ever drove under the influence of alcohol. Tom had a few fender benders and one time someone backed into the side of his car while he was at a movie. None of the accidents seemed to be related to alcohol. George paid for the car to be repaired each time.

Tom barely graduated from high school. He had been accepted at a small private college on a provisional basis. George knew Tom was intelligent and hoped he would apply himself once he was away from his high school friends, many of whom were not college bound.

As you are anticipating, but George was not, Tom flunked out of college after his freshman year. When George visited the dean of students to be sure that Tom could not be given an extension on his provisional acceptance status, he was informed of Tom's undesirable behavior. Tom had not attended class regularly and had dropped courses. He had participated in destructive fraternity

pranks, accumulated numerous unpaid parking fines, and
had been placed on probation for drinking in the dormitory. He was also responsible for causing significant damage to his dormitory. George left the campus with Tom
following him in the new car George had given him for
high school graduation. It was a sad, lonely drive for
George. He had plenty of time to review all the times he
had given and given in too much.

Tom has been to a drug treatment center. He attends
Alcoholics Anonymous (AA) meetings regularly and has a
job (not with George's company). George also attends Al-
Anon (an organization for the loved ones of alcoholics)
meetings and is trying to be a different kind of parent for
his younger daughter.

In reading about and studying parents like George who
have an extreme need to give and give in, one wonders
what is at the heart of their problem. Is it caused by a
misperception of their roles as parents or by an intrinsic
need to be loved? It is the latter—an authentic, innate
need for love—which leads them to misunderstand their
role as parents.

These parents often display this tendency with only
one of their children—the one on whom they focus all
their dreams. George was not able to control his excessive giving with his son, but he was able to control it with
his daughter. Not that George did not give her lavish
gifts periodically, but he did not consistently give her the
excessive presents he gave to Tom. George truly loved
his daughter, but he was simply not driven to
overindulge and spoil her with the love he had wanted
his own father to give him. He could tell his daughter no
and be firm, but his son never even had to ask because
George had already given him everything. George was

essentially experiencing a double-identity problem in his role as a father.

George also shares some traits with the parents who defend and deny. George was not guilty of defending, but he certainly denied reality on a number of occasions. When George considered the possessions of other boys Tom's age, he denied the inappropriateness of his gifts. Furthermore, when George did look at the things Tom's friends had, he probably cataloged the items his son didn't have because truly excessive givers are always looking for gifts they might have overlooked in their shopping sprees.

George also was in denial about the numerous changes in Tom's behavior after he turned sixteen. Just one or two of those changes would have concerned a parent who was not obsessed with giving and giving in.

Even though George was a parent in denial for many years, I credit and applaud his acceptance of the facts as outlined by the dean of students. George took action and responsibility for his part in Tom's college failure, and with great self-control, he did not defend or rescue Tom. Much to George's credit, he made some drastic changes in his relationship with his son and allowed Tom to suffer the consequences of an irresponsible lifestyle. For these reasons George is not a parent who defends and denies.

Few parents will clearly fall into only one type of parenting style. Parents who give and give in have more in common with parents who defend and deny. Both of these types of parents fear the loss of love but in different ways. However, the more a parent's behavior is aligned with one type of pattern, the less likely the parent is to practice the habits of another destructive parenting style.

Fears and Reactions of Parents Who Give and Give In

What makes parents express their love by giving and giving in to their children? People enter their maternal or paternal roles with differing family experiences. They may have grown up in a loving or an abusive home. They may have lived with both biological parents, with a single parent, in a blended family (step-family), with a relative, in a foster home, or with one or two adoptive parents. A parent may have experienced racial discrimination or enjoyed a so-called "privileged" life. The fact is, no two parents, or even siblings, experience identical rearing, and parents from all walks of life share the parenting style that I call "giving and giving in."

If no one has an identical childhood experience, what is the factor that predisposes parents to express their love by giving and giving in? The predisposition is rooted in their fear of losing their children's love. Fear of loss of love can happen in any family because it is related to how conflict was or was not handled during the parent's childhood. Most likely conflict was not handled in healthy ways by their own parents. Either expressing anger was not acceptable or anger was displayed indiscriminately and destructively.

People who grew up in homes where anger was forbidden or misused are inclined to act in ways that would avoid anger. If there is no conflict, no anger will be expressed. By giving and giving in, parents can easily evade conflict and thereby elude their children's anger. And if anger is not expressed, the parents feel that there is no threat of losing their children's love.

It is the fear of loss of love that is at the heart of the problem for parents who give and give in. Their fear of angering, or even disappointing, their children is rooted in a more general and all-encompassing fear of loss of love. Overly giving parents believe that their children cannot be angry with them and still love them.

The typical thought process of this kind of parent would be: "If I please my child, or make her happy with this gift, my child will like me and love me." The logic then progresses one step further: "If I give in just one more time, she will love me and want to act better. Or if I buy her this item, she will show gratitude by always loving me and being nice to me, and by not asking for more."

This sounds totally illogical, but it is logical to parents who give and give in because their reasoning has been skewed by fear. Remember this is a parent who has a deeply rooted fear which has been growing since childhood. The fear has evolved into the belief that people they love will leave them if angered. At this point fear of abandonment and fear of losing love have become entwined.

A parent who is reacting to a child who she fears will not love her will be unassertive. She will be reluctant to make rules and even more reluctant to enforce them. This parent will not stand up for herself; her needs will be met last. Moreover, her family may not even recognize her needs.

Another reaction will be indecision. The parent will want to please everybody all the time. It will often be difficult to make a decision which will please her child as well as her spouse. To compensate, she becomes a skilled negotiator and diplomat. She mentally rehearses how she is going to explain an unpleasant situation, dreading the reaction of her child and her spouse. This parent is hesitant to speak her mind or offer a solution because it might elicit an unfavorable reaction.

Often the parent reacts like a child. She feels she is dependent on both her spouse and her child. In many ways she does depend on them because she needs a lot of emotional support. Their moods and their demands define her role in life, and failing to please them could leave her feeling abandoned and unloved.

Parents who give and give in are generous to a fault. Their generosity can be both in time and material things. Saying no is so terribly painful for them that they often fulfill requests that have not even been verbalized. These parents are excellent at anticipating everyone's needs and desires but their own.

If the child becomes angry and the parent cannot change or stop it, the parent will withdraw. Fighting back would be foreign to her. Instead of getting mad, the parent might become distraught, but the safest reaction would be to leave the room in order to calm down and try to figure a way to extinguish the child's anger. Not surprisingly, the parent will focus on the child's feelings to the exclusion of her own.

Being steadfast and loyal, however, is their strongest reaction. Believing that if they rock the boat, they themselves will be thrown overboard, these parents are driven to give and give in too much, in order to create a bond with their children that they believe can never be broken.

Making Positive Changes

It is never too late to change, but the longer you wait the harder it is. Parents who have been giving and giving in too much for too long a time will need professional support and will only gain necessary insight through counseling.

If you think this is just a tendency and not a way of life for you, setting a few goals for change is a good way to begin. First choose one way of reacting that you want to change, such as your inability to say no, and stick to it.

Another place to start would be to develop some independence. This could be learning to take responsibility for your own happiness. Begin this change by not allowing your child's mood to influence your mood. Give yourself encouraging messages, such as, "I am having a great day and I am not going to let this pouting child drag me down."

Look at the decisions you are reluctant to make. Decide to decide. Try making some small decisions without thinking a lot about how others will react. Announce your decision with a sound of authority. You may convince both you and your child that you mean what you say by simply speaking with conviction. To your eight-year-old you might say, "I have decided to stop nagging you about putting your dirty clothes in the hamper. I will just wash what is put in the hamper and let you decide what you will do with the dirty clothes on your floor."

Add a sense of determination to your parenting style. Start by making just one rule and enforcing it consistently. Call a good friend when you are successful or when you are thinking about backing down. Ask that friend to be your cheerleader and not your critic. When you have enforced the one rule with determination and confidence for a week, add a second rule.

Warmth and sensitivity are intrinsic qualities for you. All of these newly developed parenting skills will never damage those loving traits. But being more assertive, independent, decisive, and determined will improve your self-esteem. When you are a loving but stronger parent, your child will learn to be a responsible and caring person, with an equally strong self-esteem.

Could You Be an Overloving Parent Who Gives and Gives In?

Read the following statements. The more openly and honestly you respond to each statement, the more you will learn—whether you are or could be a parent who gives and gives in too much or another kind of parent who misuses love—about your own parenting style. Respond with yes, no, or sometimes.

1. I try very hard to avoid conflict.
2. If someone is angry at me, it scares me.
3. I am a good listener.
4. I feel the most worthwhile when I am helping others.
5. I will put my friends' needs before my own.
6. My family says I am too sensitive.
7. I fear being left by those I love.
8. I feel like a failure when I can't make someone happy.

If you have five or more yes responses, you are probably a parent who gives and gives in too much. If you have four yes responses and four sometimes responses, you have the tendency to be a parent who gives and gives in too much. If you have answered no to several items, you are probably not a parent who gives and gives in. Read on to determine which parenting style is yours.

Parents Who Push and Punish

David Elkind was the first to draw national attention to the problem of parents who push and program their children in his bestselling book, *The Hurried Child*. His most recent book, *All Grown Up and No Place To Go*, continues to discuss his concern with the pressures parents place on their teenagers. Elkind warns us of the consequences of such pressures: teenage crime, drug abuse, psychological problems, and suicide.

When parents seek my advice, I am often surprised by the unrelenting schedules they have organized for their children. Could a child six or seven years old really enjoy participating in a different activity every day after school?

A hypothetical consultation with a parent who typically pushes might begin with the parent's complaint. For example, suppose a mother (whom I will call Paula) complained to me that her seven-year-old daughter wanted to stop taking piano lessons, even though she was quite talented and had loved piano last year. Wondering if her daughter's desire to quit piano was just a symptom of a bigger problem, I began: "It must be very disappointing to have a child who is talented and yet uninterested in piano. Has something else distracted or replaced her interest? Or could there be a problem with her piano teacher?"

Paula replied, "Nancy has lots of interests but none of them conflicts with her piano lessons or practice. Her piano teacher has been terrific too. She recognized Nancy's gift for music when Nancy began at four. Her teacher even recommended Nancy cut back on her practice time from fifty minutes to thirty minutes each day. She really does not want to lose one of her best pupils. She was the first to be concerned about Nancy's change of attitude."

"Tell me about her other interests," I asked.

Paula recited Nancy's schedule: "Monday is gymnastics, Tuesday is piano, Wednesday is soccer, Thursday is Blue Birds, Friday is piano again, and Saturday we have a soccer game. Of course we go to church and Sunday School on Sunday. I guess she enjoys Blue Birds the most—her best friends are also in it. Nancy does her homework after she gets home from her afternoon activity. Sometimes she finishes before dinner. She has time to practice piano before bedtime, because we do not allow television on school nights."

I commented, "That is quite a packed schedule. I'm wondering how Nancy is doing in school."

Paula boasted, "Nancy is at a private college preparatory school. She is quite bright and near the top of her class. She has never been a problem in school. Her teachers have always raved about her behavior and intelligence. The only negative comment at the teacher conference this year was that she gets her feelings hurt easily and cries easily. I was not surprised because she has been more prone to crying at home too. She has been moody and it is so easy to hurt her feelings."

I asked, "What do you do when she gets her feelings hurt and cries?"

Paula replied, "I just send her to her room until she can find her smiling face."

"How long does it take for her to 'find her smiling face'?" I asked.

Paula calculated, "Sometimes it takes Nancy twenty minutes to regain her composure; other times it may take a few hours. She never questions my order to go to her room. She accepts punishment well."

Advice for Paula: A Parent Who Pushes Too Much

Nancy was more than burned out on piano, she was completely burned out. She was a classic example of a child who was hurried. Nancy was doing too much for most seven-year-olds. In fact, most seven-year-olds cannot handle as much activity as six-year-olds.

David Elkind explains this in his book, *A Sympathetic Understanding of the Child*, by writing, "In a sense, one might even say that while at age six the child's activities were physical and motor, at age seven they become increasingly mental. It is not that the seven-year-old is less active than she was at six but rather that the scene of action has shifted and now takes place within her mind rather than within her action space."

I told Paula, "Seven is an extremely sensitive age. I am not surprised that Nancy is crying more and getting her feelings hurt more easily. Such behavior is typical for seven-year-olds. However, just because it is predictable for seven, it is not to be ignored. Seven may be sadder and moodier than six, but seven should still be fun.

"Nancy's activities for the most part are competitive and demanding. I am not surprised that Blue Birds is her favorite activity because it is basically carefree and fun, devoid of pressure and competition. She gets to play with her girlfriends in a safe and supervised atmosphere. They wear the same uniform so she feels like them. They make crafts which are not difficult, sing songs, and go on fun outings.

"I would look at gymnastics, soccer, and piano and eliminate one of them from her schedule. All three are great activities for a seven-year-old, but definitely overwhelming when combined. I suggest you ask Nancy which one she enjoys the most. Tell her you are concerned about her doing too much. Explain that although you want her to experience many different activities, to learn new skills, and to develop her talents, most of all, you want her to be happy."

Paula interrupted, asking, "What if she says she likes soccer the best. Am I suppose to let her just quit piano and gymnastics?"

I answered her question by asking, "Whose idea was it for her to take piano, gymnastics, and soccer this year?"

"Well I suggested gymnastics and soccer, and she thought they sounded like fun. I assumed she would continue the piano because she is so good at it and has always liked it," Paula explained.

"Sometimes activities sound like fun to seven-year-olds, but they have no concept of the necessary commitment and the loss of free time to just do whatever they want. Even if an elementary school age child comes to you and wants to take up a sport, she imagines herself being immediately great at the sport. She cannot imagine the frustration of being unable to do a basic skill. She does not anticipate having to practice something over and over again, or having to sit on the bench while her team loses.

"Since these activities were not her idea and she had no concept of the time commitment, my answer is yes; if she wants to play soccer and give up playing the piano, you should let her. But I do not believe that has to be the first or only solution.

"I suggest you introduce Nancy to compromise and problem solving. If you begin as I have suggested by sharing with Nancy that you are aware that she is not happy and perhaps that one of the causes is that *you* have committed her to too many activities, then you and Nancy can begin the process of finding an answer you both can live with."

Parents like Paula must learn to compromise and problem solve before they can help their children make better choices. See page 61 for more information about how you can compromise and problem solve with your child.

Paula's Approach to Punishment

Not all parents who push will punish in a physical or excessive way. Paula is one of those types of punishers. Sending Nancy to her room "until she can find her smiling face," does not seem abusive or excessive. But the problem is that this is a punishment, not a consequence.

Remember that a consequence teaches a child a lesson, a punishment does not. The only lesson Nancy learned is that she cannot have negative or unpleasant feelings. She knows that if she does feel unhappy, her home is not a safe place to share those feelings.

The other flaw with Paula's punishment for Nancy's display of sadness or frustration, is that it allows Paula to cast blame or guilt on Nancy whenever she displays feelings that Paula thinks are inappropriate. Tears are evidently unacceptable to Paula, and Nancy is shamed by being sent to her room for several hours sometimes until she can control her feelings.

Again, it is important to realize that while Paula reacts negatively to Nancy's wish to quit piano and punishes Nancy for crying, she loves Nancy very much. But it is love from a mother who uses pushing and punishing as her way of achieving what she thinks is helping her daughter. This kind of love is demanding and often impatient. It comes from the belief that she is doing the best for her child, even if it forces her into denying her child's feelings.

Paula may appear to be very different from Pat, the father introduced in Chapter 1 and further examined in this chapter, because she seems less punitive and more successful. Certainly Paula's child is more of an overachiever than Pat's. This fact frees Paula to be less punishing than Pat and enables her to feel more successful. But Paula has many of the same values, strengths, weaknesses, and fears as Pat. Unfortunately, many parents have the same character traits and parenting style as Paula and Pat. Turn to the quiz at the end of this chapter to find out if you are one of them.

Pat: A Chronic Overpunishing Parent

Pat, an agitated father of five-year-old Jason, called me on the Cope television program to complain about his "difficulties" with his son. Pat's complaints about Jason, were that Jason was strong-willed, overly energetic, and constantly trying to make him angry. Pat was concerned that Jason would "never amount to anything" and had resolved to "shape him up." Pat wanted my ideas on making Jason respect his authority.

Before I could respond to Pat's request, which sounded more like a challenge, I needed more information. Pat's initial statement led me to believe that he was a parent who pushes and punishes, however, I had yet to hear any expression of love. This failure to express love is not unusual for a parent who pushes and punishes, but it does not mean the parent does not love his child. On the contrary, when asked to explain their concern or the harsh actions, parents who push and punish will always justify their parenting behavior as an action of deep love for their children.

Pat was no different. When asked to explain his fear that Jason would be unsuccessful and his decision to set Jason on the right track, without hesitation he explained it was because he loved Jason very much. He reiterated that whatever he did he did out of love and for Jason's own good. I wondered if Jason would agree someday that his father's punishing him had really worked for his own good. I also doubted that Jason would ever feel the love his father was using to justify his parenting technique.

Jason was Pat's first-born and his only son. Pat said that he knew how hard it was to make it in this world. He rationalized that if Jason did not obey him then he would never obey his teachers. If he did not obey his teachers, he would be a failure in school and in life. This type of leap-frog logic is typical of parents who push and punish. They see cause and effect relationships in everything. They begin to believe that one mistake will ruin a person's life. They begin with a specific fear and expand it to global proportions, arriving at conclusions such as "he will never amount to anything."

I agreed with Pat that children must first learn to obey and respect their parents before they can learn to obey and respect their teachers. But I did not agree with Pat's method of teaching respect and obedience. What Pat was expecting from Jason was closer to military obedience. I learned more about Pat's ideas on respect and his methods of teaching respect when I asked him to give me some examples of something Jason would do that was disobedient. Remember Jason was only five.

Pat replied, "One thing that really irritates me is that he won't sit still. At the dinner table he will swing his legs. He will play with his knife and fork. He will fidget and often spill something. I am constantly on him to straighten up, keep his hands in his lap, and sit still. He knows how I feel about how he acts at the table, but he does it anyway. It is like he is trying to bug me.

"Jason also leaves his toys all over the house. He never puts anything up before he gets out something else. I find pieces to puzzles or parts of games in the family room. He knows the rules about picking up after himself, but I'm always having to punish him to teach him a lesson about minding me."

I asked Pat, "What kind of punishment do you use when Jason leaves his toys out or doesn't sit still at the dinner table?"

Pat replied, "I don't spank him that much. I usually have him stand facing the wall with his arms extended straight out to the side. But even then he doesn't stand still. He will let his arms drop a little. He is supposed to stand still for thirty minutes with his arms out. When he drops his arms at all, I make him hold one of my shoes in each of his hands with his arms extended to teach him to mind me."

"Does he mind you then?" I asked.

"No," Pat explained, "he will shift his weight from one foot to another and maybe start sniffling. It really makes me mad that he won't mind. What I want you to tell me is how I can make him respect me and obey me and my rules."

Learning More About Pat

Pat had to be persuaded to examine his parenting style so he could realize that it was not working. Only then would he be ready to consider making some changes in his expectations, rules, discipline, and methods of building self-esteem.

"Before I answer your question, Pat, I am curious about your childhood and the way you were raised," I began as nonthreateningly as possible.

Pat responded, "My father was in the military. We moved around a lot. My mother taught school. The kids were taught to keep house, to cook, and to obey their parents. When we did something wrong, we were given a whipping we would remember. We learned quickly to not do anything wrong. Except my younger brother, who never learned. He and my parents would go 'round and 'round. He was hard headed and a fighter."

"What happened to your brother?" I asked.

"He ran away at fifteen, and we never heard from him again," Pat replied in a softer voice. "He was just not up to living under their strict rules. I thought my parents were strict, but I believed it was for our own good. I lived by their rules. It wasn't pleasant, but I turned out pretty well. I have been successful. And I want to be successful with Jason."

I probed a little further. "Do you see much of your parents now?"

"No," Pat explained, "when my parents retired, they moved to Florida (where Pat also lived). But we don't get along well. We have not seen them in years."

I asked, "Pat, do you want to be a different kind of father than your father?"

Pat intensely retorted, "I am nothing like my father. My father overdisciplined me. His whippings were more like beatings. I would never hurt Jason. I love Jason."

I responded, "I sincerely believe you. But I also must be honest with you. I consider the punishment you have described as extreme. I also believe you are trying to be a good parent to Jason. However, when you have been raised in a harsh, perhaps abusive way, it is very difficult to be the kind of parent you want to be.

"Parents raise their children pretty much the way their own parents raised them, even if they hated the way they were raised. For most of us, our parents serve as the only models on parenting we have. As children, we may have decided we were going to do things differently when we became parents, but we never received the parenting training that would enable us to do so. We just have mental tapes of how our parents reared us. When we are under stress, these tapes play back our parents' responses, and we find ourselves doing or saying the very things we promised ourselves we would *never* say or do. Or we may not communicate and act in exactly the same ways, but the results are the same. We have changed enough to look and sound differently, but not enough to make a difference in our children's lives.

"This does not mean we cannot change significantly or we cannot be better parents. It just takes learning some new ways of parenting. I believe you can be a more successful parent." I told Pat that I believed he and Jason could have a better relationship than they had now, certainly a much better relationship than Pat had with his own father. I asked Pat if he would be willing to consider loving Jason in a different way, and if he would be willing to look at and think about Jason in a different way. Pat said he'd like to try.

In response I began, "Parenting is never easy and it is definitely harder with some children than it is with others. Sometimes that is because the child is so much like you. Other times it may be difficult because the child is so different from you. Also parenting can be the most difficult when you do not know what behavior to expect from the child, especially if your expectations are unrealistic. Having unrealistic expectations means thinking that the child is capable of acting and thinking more maturely than he can. Consequently, both you and your child are set up for failure.

"I think Jason is very different from you. Moreover, I believe you have unrealistic expectations for him. So you are trying to be a successful parent with two strikes against you. But your personality differences and your unrealistic expectations are also two strikes against Jason. You do not understand him and you think he is capable of behaving on a much more mature level than he can.

"Instead of trying to change Jason and make him more like you, I am suggesting you begin to look at what you like about Jason that is not like you. At first you may not be able to think of anything, but if you really think about it, you will begin to see some positive characteristics in Jason. Until you do, Jason will not feel good about himself. He knows that you want him to be better, but he does not think he can ever live up to what you want in a son.

"There is an important parenting rule that applies to your situation: A misbehaving child is a discouraged child. Jason is a discouraged child. He does not believe in himself and he will not believe in himself until he thinks you believe in him. So you must start looking for something Jason does well. It may be the way he smiles or the way he loves a pet. Whatever it is, it is up to you to find it. This will be hard for you because your expectations are so high.

"Let's talk about expectations. The behaviors you described to me—being unable to sit still, being messy, and leaving his toys out—are all typical of a five-year-old child. I suspect his fidgeting is caused by nervousness. He is just waiting for you to become angry with him. He knows he frustrates and disappoints you. No wonder he makes mistakes. No wonder he spills things. Anticipating your negative reaction prompts him to conduct himself the only way he knows how—through intensified age-appropriate behavior.

"The form of punishment you have described, having Jason stand with his arms extended straight out from his side for thirty minutes, is severe punishment, inappropriate for any age, and abusive. In addition, it has not worked, as you have admitted, and it has not taught Jason any lesson but to fear you. When you add to the punishment by having him hold one of your shoes in each hand, you are only increasing the cruelty of the punishment; you are not increasing the chance that Jason will mind you. On the contrary, because of his fear of you, it is more likely he will slip up and make another mistake. Failure breeds low self-esteem. Low self-esteem sets the stage for failure, and the cycle goes on and on.

"I realize that you did not consider this punishment abusive or you certainly would not have used it. I understand that you were punished even more severely when you were a boy. I am sure you decided then that you would never hurt your child the way your father hurt you. Instead, you chose a punishment that did not seem to be physically painful—especially when compared with the beatings you received. But the punishment you chose has caused Jason physical pain. In addition it is emotionally painful because it sets Jason up for failure. It is impossible for a child his age to stand that way for ten minutes, much less thirty minutes. It was a harsh punishment, not an effective discipline."

To Pat's credit he listened to everything I had to say. He seemed slightly skeptical at first, but eventually sounded convinced of the benefits of using discipline instead of punishment. But Pat worried that if he eased his strict rules, Jason would think he had won. I suggested that Pat prepare Jason by telling him he wanted to be a different kind of father. I even encouraged Pat to share briefly his desire to have a better relationship with Jason than he had had with his own father.

For a child like Jason the change will be uncomfortable, even though it is a positive change, until he believes that his "new dad" is there to stay. Therefore Pat should expect Jason to test his commitment to the new relationship. Jason had already learned how to respond to the "old" Pat, and it would take time, trial, and error before he learned how to respond to the new.

I concluded my conversation with Pat by urging him to take a parenting class, explaining that the class would provide support and encouragement in changing his and Jason's lives. The parenting class would also teach him even more parenting skills.

The Difference Between Punishment and Discipline

There is a significant difference between punishment and discipline. To understand the difference, parents should know that discipline means "to teach." According to this definition, a parent realizes that disciplining or teaching can happen every day. Discipline should not be reserved for the times a child is misbehaving. As a matter of fact, it is most effective when a child is being good. Ideally a parent's goal is to build a child's self-esteem to the point where the child has a realistic and positive self-image most of the time and has learned to prefer feeling good about himself. In order to perpetuate this good feeling, the child becomes self-disciplined. Then discipline can take place exclusively when the child is being good. It is much more fun and productive for both parent and child.

The problem with children like Jason is that their self-esteem is so low because they are always in trouble. For Pat, Jason won't start behaving better until Pat begins recognizing and praising his good behavior. Essentially, Jason is not capable of changing for the better until Pat changes the way he communicates with and disciplines Jason.

Punishment, not discipline, makes children feel guilty. Discipline is meant to teach children to make better choices in their behavior. Discipline places responsibility on the child to behave at an age-appropriate level. That is where realistic expectations come in. Learn what your child is physically and mentally capable of doing and expect that—nothing more and nothing less. David Elkind has written a book entitled *A Sympathetic Understanding of the Child: Birth to Sixteen* (Allyn: 1978), which explains normal social behavior and development in children and is a wonderful resource for parents.

Certainly every parent would love their five-year-old children to sit still, use good manners, and never spill anything. But it would be unrealistic for parents to expect that. Expecting perfect behavior would only open themselves to disappointment and anger, and open their children to unnecessary failure. Sitting still and using good manners are goals many parents have for their children. But reaching those goals is a process of learning, making mistakes, and trying harder. The trick is to make those skills the children's own goals, because when they succeed with their self-esteem in tact, they can take pride in their own achievement.

Discipline also involves setting a few good rules. The rules must be:

1. understandable by the child
2. age appropriate (something they can do)
3. enforceable (you know immediately when the rule is broken)

When the rule is broken, the child should be told in a calm, adult voice by the parent that she has made a bad choice. For example the parent might say, "I see you chose not to put up your toy." Having previously agreed with the child on the rules for putting away toys, the child should experience the consequence you had advised her to expect now that the rule has been disobeyed.

Consequences: The Price That Must Be Paid

The child pays a price for breaking a rule. The child knows the consequence in advance, just as she knows the rule to pick up her toys by bedtime. The parent reinforces this understanding by restating the rule and consequence whenever a rule is broken. For example, the parent might say, "You have chosen to not play with the toy tomorrow when you chose to leave it on the floor this evening. The next time you get to play with it, I know you will do better."

The parent is not the villain. The rule and consequence were known in advance and understood by the child, and the child was capable of following the rule. The child simply forgot, which is also common in young children, but something the child is capable of improving. The consequence must be enforced consistently because this prevents the child from feeling bad or guilty. The child recognizes that she made a bad choice when she chose not to pick up her toy. She also believes she will do better next time because you, her parent, said you believe she could do better.

Compromising and Problem Solving Together

Parents have a responsibility to teach children that problems do not always have just one solution, and there does not have to be just one winner and one loser in a disagreement. Children can learn about solving problems, compromise, and decision making by watching their parents, especially if their parents talk about how they solve some problems, compromise with others, or struggle with a difficult decision.

Of course parents are very selective when they choose situations to explain to their children, but lessons about problems are best learned by children when the problem is theirs and they are allowed to help find a solution and make the decision themselves. This is particularly hard for the parent to accept when the solution the child chooses is not the solution the parent would have preferred. It is, therefore, extremely important that the parent be willing to accept the child's decision and to allow the child to experience the consequences of that decision.

If Paula told Nancy she wanted her to decide what activities to eliminate from her busy schedule and Nancy chose to drop the piano lessons, Paula must not refuse to let Nancy have her choice. Otherwise, the message to Nancy would be, "you are not capable of solving your problems." Moreover, Nancy would not believe her mother the next time she offered to let Nancy make her own decision.

Problem solving begins with both the child and the parent recognizing that the child has a problem. Nancy's problem is that she is pushed and pressured by too many after-school activities. Paula should begin by expressing concern for Nancy. Then Paula should invite Nancy to express how she feels about all the different commitments she has. Paula should resist trying to direct or change what Nancy says. Paula's role is to listen and encourage Nancy to be open and honest.

The next step is to ask the child to think of all the possible solutions. Here Paula should offer Nancy the chance to think of as many ways as she could to make her schedule more fun and less stressful. At this point it is difficult for a parent like Paula to resist reacting adversely to some of the solutions that her child might give. However, to do a good job of teaching problem solving, Paula should ask what other ideas Nancy has without making negative comments about the ideas she does not like.

After all the ideas have been listed by the child, the parent should ask the child to consider each idea and the consequences of making that choice. For example, Paula might ask Nancy what it would feel like to give up piano lessons, if that was one of Nancy's ideas. Paula would discuss each option in this way without giving her own opinion. Remember the child, not the mother, is learning to make a decision.

In reviewing options the child will eliminate some of her ideas because she realizes that she does not like the consequence attached to the idea. Now the child should be able to narrow down the choices, ideally, to one or two solutions. A final decision does not have to be made at this time. It is often beneficial to suggest that the child take a few days to see if she really wants to follow through with her idea. Nancy may not know whether she wants to give up both gymnastics and piano. After thinking it over for a few days, she may compromise by giving up gymnastics and just one day of piano lessons.

Making a commitment to try the chosen solution for a reasonable period of time is the next step. For Nancy this might be until the end of the school year. Nancy and Paula would agree to re-examine the plan when summer began. By then they would be able to tell if Nancy felt good about her decision, if it had relieved stress, and if she wanted to make any changes when school began again.

This is a proven method of problem solving. When the child does not make the best selection of solutions, the plan can be changed at the agreed review time. Meanwhile, the child is learning to take responsibility for what she does. The parent must resist saying such things as, "I could have told you this would happen" or "I knew you would be sorry." The consequence teaches the lesson and the parent's critical remarks only detract from the power of the consequence.

Taking this approach can be very difficult for parents like Paula who push and punish because they believe they are the only ones capable of making decisions for their children. Their child would be the last person they would trust to decide what is best.

Could You Be an Overloving Parent Who Pushes and Punishes?

Read the following statements. The more openly and honestly you respond to each statement, the more you will learn—whether you are or could become a parent who pushes and punishes or another kind of parent who misuses love—about your parenting style. Respond with yes, no, or sometimes.

1. I try very hard when I am in a leadership position.
2. I can make decisions quickly.
3. I am good at motivating others.
4. I enjoy being self-reliant.
5. I do not tolerate incompetence well.
6. People who are weak or indecisive irritate me.
7. My advice is usually taken.
8. I feel successful in most aspects of my life.
9. I like being in charge.
10. I admire someone who can accomplish many things.

If you have six or more yes responses, you are probably a parent who pushes and punishes too much. If you have four yes responses and four sometimes responses, you have the tendency to be a parent who pushes and punishes too much. If you have five or more no responses, you are not a parent who pushes and punishes. Read on to determine which parenting style is yours.

Parents Who Criticize
and Control

A biological parent cannot choose his child, but a parent who criticizes and controls is trying to make his child into the child he would have chosen if given the opportunity. Deep down the child of a critical parent knows he is a disappointment and that he will never be the child of his parent's dream. Tragically, the child keeps trying to make his parent's dream come true.

When the child becomes an adolescent, more than the typical adolescent behavior may occur. Resentment has built up and the preteen will begin to reclaim some control over the parts of his life that will irritate his controlling parent the most. Let us consider Carol, the criticizing and controlling mother of eleven-year-old Jordan.

Carol: Looking at Her Problem

Carol's cooperative ten-year-old had turned into a disappointing eleven-year-old, according to her description.

His grades had dropped. She suspected that his school friends were a bad influence. After summarizing Jordan's change in attitude and performance, Carol asked, "How can I make him take his schoolwork more seriously and not be like so many kids today who never work hard or learn to make some sacrifices now so they can be prepared for the future?"

Notice how a controlling person like Carol asks a question. It is never a general question like, "Can you help me?" Instead the question is always very specific and includes guidelines to prevent the counselor from responding in a direction the person might not want to explore. Carol's question also gave her the opportunity to state her opinion about what is wrong with today's youth. Criticizing parents always have an opinion that they are more than willing to share.

Carol's question felt like a command performance for me. She was dictating the direction of the consultation, but I was not ready to play the role she had designed for me. So I responded with a question instead of the answer she was likely not to accept.

"Are you the kind of person who is very organized and efficient?" I countered.

"Well, yes. Why do you ask?" Carol replied defensively.

I explained to Carol that parents who are efficient, organized, and in control of their lives, are often frustrated when they cannot have the same conditions in their roles as parents. I asked Carol, "Wouldn't you like to have the same sense of confidence about your control of Jordan's future as you do of your own?"

Carol responded, "Well of course, wouldn't all parents like that?"

I told her that she would be surprised. Not all parents

expect that degree of control. Moreover, they do not even want to control their children's future. That is not to say that these parents don't have hopes and dreams for their children. They also try to be a positive influence in their children's lives. They teach their values and moral beliefs. They share their opinions, feelings, and thoughts with their children. These parents also have fears for their children. So they set limits and boundaries, give them guidelines, and enforce rules. But in the end they know that with each passing year they will have less control over their children's lives. And having less control is okay with them. "Does that way of parenting seem reasonable to you?" I asked her.

Carol explained, "I don't want to always have control over Jordan. My goal is for him to be self-disciplined. But he is only eleven. You can't possibly be recommending that I leave important decisions such as what level of schoolwork he should be doing or what friends would be good for Jordan for him to decide on his own. Jordan has no comprehension of how important those decisions are. His schoolwork is already inconsistent. His taste in friends is highly questionable."

"You are not going to like my advice," I said, "but I recommend exactly what you cannot imagine. I think Jordan's schoolwork is just that—Jordan's schoolwork. It is not yours. It belongs to him, if you will let it belong to him. You have been to school once and now it is his turn. Before you discount my recommendation, let me explain.

"Jordan is a bright eleven-year-old boy who is in early adolescence. Now that he has entered adolescence he is not going to accept your attempts to control him. Even though he has been a very cooperative, complacent child in the past, his hormones are telling him he is not a little boy anymore. You may think that he is still a child and some days he will too. But more frequently he will feel too mature to be told what to do and how to think.

"The more you criticize and control, the more Jordan will resist. For Jordan to accept your advice, he must see a change in your attitude toward him. He needs to think that you think he is capable of making some decisions for himself.

"I suggest that you give up some control. If you do that, you will be able to retain the most essential control. I must warn you that if you do not make some changes in your critical and controlling parenting style, you are pushing Jordan toward more serious rebellion. The choice is yours to make."

"I don't want to make a choice like that," Carol stated. "I do not trust his judgment at this age, but I do not want his rebellious attitude to continue. What if his grades continue to drop? What if he gets in the wrong crowd in middle school? Can you guarantee me that if I let go of some control, he will make the right choices?"

"No, I can make no promises as to what Jordan will choose to do," I admitted. "However, I can make some predictions. My predictions are based on what you have told me about yourself and Jordan and are founded in my understanding of child development."

Adolescent Development and Needs

There are five tasks adolescents must accomplish before they can become happy, responsible adults. While all of them are equally important, some children and their parents may have more trouble accomplishing one of the tasks than they have with the others. For Carol and Jordan, and for many other parents and their children, it is the fifth task that is so problematic.

Adolescent Development Tasks

1. **Develop a sexual identity**—Associated behavior would range from interest in grooming products to dating.

2. **Attain personality integration**—Associated behavior would involve trying different roles, such as intellectual, class clown, or athlete.

3. **Choose a career goal**—Begins with the child talking about what he or she wants to be, and ends with the adolescent achieving the education necessary for the chosen career.

4. **Clarify and accept values**—Begins with early adolescent acceptance of parents' values and beliefs, changes to challenging and sometimes rejecting parents' values and beliefs, and finally ends in late adolescence with the child accepting most of the values and beliefs with which he or she was raised.

5. **Separate from parents**—This is probably the most difficult of all of the developmental tasks for the parents of adolescents. And unfortunately it is the task that plays a significant role in the other four tasks, because children who do not separate from their parents cannot be totally successful in the other four challenges.

Some of the behaviors that indicate your adolescent is trying to separate from you are:

- shutting their bedroom door

- having private telephone conversations

- not satisfactorily answering your questions about their school experiences, friends, activities, feelings, or thoughts

- choosing their own clothes

- not doing something the first time you ask them to do it

- staying home while the rest of the family goes out

- ignoring your sage advice

- being critical of you

- not talking as much at meal times

- not trying to please you

The list of separating activities is much longer, but these are some of the most common ones. If your child displays any of these behaviors, you should take it as warning signs that he or she may be trying to create some physical and emotional distance.

It is important for parents to view these changes as not only normal, but necessary. Whether the adolescent is a boy or a girl, an overachiever or an underachiever, your child needs to separate from you before he or she can become a happy, productive, responsible, and likeable adult.

Separating is hard on both the parent and the child. There is never a simple, clean break. It is more like a slow tearing apart. It happens over years. Some parents are more prepared for the break than others. Some adolescents achieve the separation in less drastic or hurtful ways. Parents can usually determine how successful or constructive the separation is by allowing their teenagers to feel some independence before they accomplish the break through drastic steps.

Parent-Child Separation: The Necessary Step

Therapists Marion Sue Jones and John De Fore once described the process of allowing children to grow up to be independent and responsible like this: When you bring an infant home from the hospital, you place him in a crib. This bed provides safe boundaries, preventing him from falling out. You know right where your baby is even when you are not in his room.

When your child is crawling and even toddling, you shut doors to some rooms, limiting the safe places he can wander. You put dangerous or breakable things out of his reach. He now has more space to wander and have fun. You have expanded his world.

When your child is big enough to play outside unattended, you may let him play in a fenced backyard. He has rules such as not trying to climb out of the yard or digging in the flower bed. If he breaks one of the rules, he cannot play outside for awhile, until you feel he has earned your trust again. You expect him to test rules and you are prepared to enforce the consequences.

Then your child becomes old enough to ride a bike. At first he rides with your supervision. Sooner than you think, he is capable of riding to a friend's house on your block. He has earned your trust, so you expand his world again by giving him the privilege of riding his bike to the friend's house. He is expected to call when he gets there and when he is ready to come home. When he breaks the rule, you give him the previously agreed on and understood consequences of putting away his bike for a couple of days. His world is temporarily smaller. He will value and more responsibly enjoy the privilege of riding his bike beyond his home when he earns another chance.

Soon he is mature enough to spend the night with a friend. He may even be ready to go to camp. There are a few good rules to go with the chances to expand his world of freedom. He earns more trust as he demonstrates his trustworthiness. You continue to increase the responsibility and freedom he has at each age and stage of development.

Before you are ready, he is sixteen and has a driver's license. However, if you have continually increased your teen's independence as he accepted the accompanying responsibilities, your fears are somewhat eased by the knowledge that he has been thoroughly trained to handle independence and freedom responsibly.

With a set of car keys, your child's world has significantly expanded. It may be the police and not you who enforces the rules. If your child chooses to speed, and hopefully is caught, the consequence is a traffic ticket. But you also will have a consequence for his failure to make a responsible choice: the car keys are taken away for a previously agreed amount of time. His world is temporarily smaller until your trust is earned again.

How can it be time for your child to leave for college? It seems like just yesterday he was learning to ride his bike. Is he prepared to manage this new freedom? Probably more prepared than most because you have done your job of allowing him constructive ways to separate. He has experienced, at increasing degrees of trust, freedom and independence at appropriate ages. You have gradually relinquished your job as he demonstrated willingness and capability of assuming the role. You will be sad, you will have fears, but your instincts will tell you that your child is prepared for the challenges, responsibilities, and fun of independent living. At this point you both know that you have done a good job of separating.

Parenting is the only job I know where you are trying to work yourself out of a job. The goal of parenting is to raise happy, independent, and responsible adults. So parenting at its best is the constant process of deparenting.

Carol's Reaction

After explaining the adolescent developmental tasks and the corresponding theories about raising independent and responsible children to Carol, I asked her, "How do you feel about what I have just explained to you?"

"I must admit I see your point," Carol began, "but I just don't think it will work for Jordan."

"Do you mean that it won't work for Jordan or it won't work for you?" I asked.

"Since you put it that way, it probably won't work for either one of us," Carol admitted.

"Your instincts are probably right," I affirmed. "You know yourself and Jordan better than anyone. Do you want to make any changes? Do you think you can let go of some of your control?"

"Yes," Carol said, "what you have said makes sense. I see the importance of separating from Jordan. But I don't trust his judgment because I have never given him the chance to make his own decisions. It is true that I don't want him to make any mistakes so I have always told him what to do. But it is because I love him and want the best for him. I believe years from now he will thank me for keeping him on the right path. Yet I can see now that I have got to prepare him for when I am not around to lead him and advise him. I will try to find some places to let go. But schoolwork is not a place to begin. Jordan's grades and participation in honors classes are too important to his future."

If Carol were to improve her relationship with her son, she would have to find the courage to let Jordan make some mistakes while the prices are not too high. But when critical and controlling parents receive different advice than what they had expected, they tend to become critical and to discount that advice. The use of "yes . . . but" is common for critical controllers. No matter what the suggestion is, the critical controller will reply, "yes . . . but" to explain why the idea won't work. It becomes a futile exercise to continue trying to recommend a solution or new way of doing something. A "yes . . . but" parent is not really seeking advice, but affirmation that he or she is doing the right thing, or that there is no solution to the problem.

Like many criticizing and controlling parents, Carol's ego was involved. Carol was not so much concerned for Jordan as she was for herself. She was afraid of losing the respect and admiration of others. How would it look and what would others think? When Jordan grows up, he may question who enjoyed his childhood more—himself or his mother. And before he is grown, while he is a teenager, he will very likely express his feelings more than once by saying, "It's my life! Leave me alone!"

Unfortunately, if Carol finds some area of Jordan's life that she will allow him to control, she will disapprove of his decisions and probably try to influence them. A critical person can always see ways to improve another's plans. Sadly, critical people always find imperfection in their own work as well. Because of this, it is hard for them to ever relax or enjoy life.

Cathy: How Her Parenting Style Affected Her Mother-Daughter Relationships

Cathy was a typical mother asking for advice about handling her children, particularly one who would not keep her room clean. As we talked about her efforts to get her daughter, Susie, to keep her room neat and tidy, I became aware that this was a battle Cathy was not likely to win. I also observed that the true casualty of their war was Susie's older sister, Jane.

Cathy openly and proudly admitted she was a perfectionist. She believed everything had a place and belonged in its place. She also believed children had a place and belonged in it as well. Cathy made clear that she believed a child's place was wherever she thought the child should be, doing whatever she thought the child should be doing at that moment.

Jane was easily parented, according to Cathy. Jane was obedient, self-entertained, organized, and very neat. Then there was Susie. From the beginning Susie would not cooperate with Cathy. She resisted feeding schedules as an infant. She threw tantrums as a toddler and seemed hard-headed when she didn't get what she wanted. Cathy's current power struggle with Susie was over her messy room.

I asked Susie's age and inquired about her degree of messiness. Susie was six at the time of our conversation and her messiness included not putting her toys back in their places before taking out another toy, leaving dirty clothes on the floor instead of putting them in the dirty clothes hamper, and sometimes not making her bed. Cathy had no problem with Susie's older sister and was determined to change Susie's bad habits. However, she had not been successful so far.

Cathy had tried numerous punishments but nothing had worked. She wanted some fresh "ammunition" from me. But the more I heard of Cathy's rigid tone and combative words, the more I rooted for Susie. More seriously, I sympathized with both of Cathy's children, as I pictured what it would be like to live with such a critical, demanding mother.

Cathy and Susie had been locked in a series of power struggles. Cathy had currently met her match because Susie had found an issue, cleaning her room, which drove Cathy crazy. Susie could be passively aggressive by simply forgetting to make her bed or by responding very slowly to her mother's demands to clean up her room. As this scenario played out, Susie's sister, Jane, watched in horror as Cathy screamed in anger and Susie dawdled. Jane would help Susie pick up to prevent her mother from becoming angry. Jane would also try to behave even better to divert her mother's attention. This did not work because Cathy ignored her good behavior and neat habits except when using them as examples of how Susie should act.

Jane was the one who was bearing the burden of their mother's critical behavior. She felt helpless and unable to secure lasting peace in her home. She knew how to please her mother, but could not seem to teach Susie her strategy. All of her diverting maneuvers were either ignored or used as ammunition for her mother's case against Susie. Jane retreated into her shell as the war grew to include other issues, such as Susie's lack of perfection in other areas. Susie was fighting and surviving while Jane was imprisoned in her own home.

Since Cathy had tried numerous punishments, most of which were extreme, unrelated to her behavior, and all of which were unsuccessful, Cathy did not need suggestions for more consequences that would teach Susie to be more responsible. At this point, any consequence was bound to fail. The battles had become more significant than their initial reasons for fighting; by now too many feelings had been wounded and too many scars were apparent. A truce was necessary.

I asked Cathy, "How do you feel about your relationship with Susie?"

Cathy responded, "I think it is awful. How can I have a good relationship with a daughter who won't do what I say when I say it?"

I suggested, "A child is more likely to do what a parent asks if she has a good relationship with her parent. In other words, you may have the steps reversed. Improve the relationship first and then she will improve her behavior."

Cathy asked, "How long will that take and how do I do it?"

I explained, "First you have to accept Susie as she is—she is very different from you in some ways. Then love her unconditionally no matter how perfectly or imperfectly she performs. Next, learn to appreciate Susie's fighting spirit, her strong will, her more casual attitude about neatness, order, and schedules, and her unique personality. There is no one else in the world like Susie. I think I would like her. She sounds bright and fun. Yes, she has a mind of her own, but that is a strength not a weakness. I would like to have her on my team, not as my opponent. Having her in your life is a challenge, but one that I think you could learn and benefit from. Don't you wish you had stood up to or ignored some people, possibly one of your parents, at some time in your life?"

Cathy answered, "I would not have dared to disobey my parents or to ignore them, but I guess I wish sometimes I could now. But I cannot imagine it. However, I think I get your point. I would like to have a better relationship with Susie than I do. Jane and I seem to get along much better. She is just a more obedient child. She wants to please me."

I guessed, "I bet Jane is more like you were with your parents?"

Cathy agreed and added, "Maybe that's not so good either."

I told Cathy she should be concerned about Jane too, and explained that the perfect child usually does not have the privilege or pleasure of being a child. The perfect child's role is to make you proud, divert your attention from the misbehaving sibling (which is impossible), and to be the peacemaker.

Cathy asked, "Are you recommending that I allow Susie to just have a messy room and work on the relationship?"

"Yes," I replied. "Focus your attention on your relationship with your daughters not the issue of the messy room. If you put as much time and effort into your relationship with them as you put into the battle over the room, I think you will be successful and everyone will be much happier. Eventually the room will be more tidy, probably never to your standards, but better.

"Don't just drop the issue of the bedroom. Ask Susie and Jane to sit down with you and tell them you are tired of all the lecturing, reminding, coaxing, and fussing. Tell them you want to have a fresh start with them. Say you want more laughter and fun with them. Explain that you are turning over their rooms to them for awhile. Ask them to keep their rooms as pretty as *they* want them. Set a time each week to talk separately with them about how you are feeling and how they are feeling. Promise you are going to try your best to loosen up and stop being so critical, but tell them that you may make some slipups. Ask for their patience and understanding. Apologize for not always showing your love. Reassure them that you love them for who they are, not what they do. Close by saying that you cannot imagine your life without them."

Characteristics of Parents Who Criticize and Control

Parents who criticize and control appear to be terrific parents. Their children are at school on time, clean, appropriately dressed, respectful to their teachers, have a nutritious

lunch, and carry their completed homework in organized backpacks. These parents attend open house and
teacher conferences at school. They always know their
children's athletic schedules, homework assignments,
and test dates. Such parents set early bedtimes, juggle
carpools, and enforce strict curfews. They provide structure, they model responsible behavior, and they are consistent and predictable. Of course, these are all good
goals for successful parenting, but they are only good in
moderation. Obviously the criticizing and controlling
parent has many qualities and skills to be admired and
emulated, but their frequent overuse of them is not to be
commended.

What exactly is their problem? And what do these parents have in common with the other parents who love too
much? The problem is their fascination with excess; with
their "too much" way of loving. When critical and controlling parents love too much, their love is expressed by
overcriticizing and overcontrolling.

Excessive criticism and use of control becomes dogma
and rigidity. Their favorite way of doing anything is their
own way. Often they surround themselves with people
who hold the same attitudes. They do not understand
people who think differently from them, and they are not
sensitive to people who have different feelings.

With friends and coworkers, critical and controlling
people have usually learned to suppress their tendencies
to be rudely outspoken or offensively argumentative.
However, with family, and particularly with their children, these people can be uncompromising and insensitive. With their children and sometimes with their
spouses they may also be impatient, unsympathetic, and
demanding.

They are happiest with their family when everyone is on schedule, efficient, and orderly. These parents insist on respectful and polite conduct and feel in control when they get it. They tend to lecture more than talk. They listen with a critical ear, always focusing on what they need to correct or improve. It is hard for a child to feel close to this type of parent because the criticism and control keep the child at a distance and on the defensive. As a result, the parent-child relationship is tense and lacks spontaneity.

Fears of Parents Who Criticize and Control

Why do parents express their love by criticizing and controlling? Like the three other types of parents who love in destructive ways, parents who criticize and control act out of fear. It is a fear that was nourished during their own childhood. They probably had a dominant parent who was either pushing and punishing or critical and controlling. The way they avoided punishment or criticism was by learning to control their actions and words very carefully. Some of these people learned the hard way. They fought, tested, deceived, and rebelled. Others were more compliant and pleasing.

Whatever they were like as children, they learned the importance of being in control of their lives. Now, as adults and as parents, they are driven by the fear of losing that control. Criticizers and controllers often keep themselves under control by watching their diets, exercising, having routines, and staying on schedules. They operate from a list of things to do. When under stress, they will make more lists and become more compulsive in their daily routines, whether they include cleaning or exercising. Moreover, they have a place in the community, a role in their families, and a face or image to maintain. Not only do they have to control themselves, they must also control the significant people in their lives.

A parent may feel the loss of control most keenly when a child does not conform to a certain family image. If a child does not adhere to the rules, the parent may feel both an individual threat and a threat to the whole family structure he or she has worked so hard to control. The parent will analyze and judge the child's behavior and then express disapproval. The first thing to achieve is obedience, because disobedience indicates a loss of control. The second thing is improvement, because the critical parent can always see ways in which the child could do better.

Ways Criticizing and Controlling Parents Can Improve

If there were one word of advice I would give parents who criticize and control excessively, it would be, "relax." The problem is that "relaxation" is not in their vocabulary. They have forgotten how to have fun or what it is like to be a child. They probably were not allowed to be children very long, so it is only natural that they are not very good at it.

Part of relaxing is being more spontaneous. Schedules and commitments are such a big part of their lives that they do not know how they can fit spontaneity into their agendas. They need practice putting their calendars aside to spend unstructured time with the children doing things just for the fun of it.

A companion to spontaneity is flexibility. Critical and controlling parents are unbending. They have a plan that they feel compelled to stick to. Their rigid approach to their daily routines sets them up for conflict with their children because children almost always require parents to be flexible in order to maintain a happy and stress-free home. When a child does not or cannot adhere to a rigid schedule, the controlling parent gets "stressed out" and the tension in the household becomes extremely heavy. Everyone is tense and no one wins.

Next I recommend that critical and controlling parents try to be more sensitive. Because these parents were not raised with the belief that expressing their feelings is acceptable, they do not know how to identify their own feelings, much less accept the feelings of their family members. If no one ever asked them what they were feeling, they are not likely to ask themselves or anyone else. These parents would benefit tremendously from counseling, primarily because they would begin to understand their own feelings. Accomplishing that would be a major step toward accepting the feelings of their children, even when their children's feelings are very different from their own.

To change and improve their relationship with their family, it is important that they begin to appreciate the qualities and personalities that each person has. Their tendency is to be critical and even intolerant of others' differences. This only creates barriers to relationships and fosters low self-esteem in other people.

Look for uniqueness in your children and cherish it. Our children have many qualities we can learn from. Sometimes the qualities which irritate us the most are admirable in some way. Take, for example, the child who is not athletic and does not take sports as seriously as her parents. She is probably having more fun and putting less unnecessary stress on herself by choosing not to be involved in competitive sports.

Compromising is the last way to improve. Compromise makes it possible for everybody to win. But compromising is particularly difficult for critical and controlling parents because they believe that their way is the only way. This makes compromise feel like failure. Consequently, this area of improvement is a major change and challenge because it requires letting go of control over the outcome or result. The compromised solution may not feel perfect, or even efficient, but the parent-child relationship wins because control is shared.

Could You Be an Overloving Parent Who Criticizes and Controls?

Read the following statements. The more openly and honestly you respond to each statement, the more you will learn—whether you are or could become a parent who criticizes and controls or another kind of parent who misuses love—about your parenting style. Respond with yes, no, or sometimes.

1. I am good at analyzing problems.
2. I am organized and efficient.

3. I like to know what is expected of me.

4. I am angry if I am treated with disrespect.

5. Having a schedule makes me feel comfortable.

6. I am good at showing my children the best way to do things.

7. I am a hard worker.

8. Others would say I am a perfectionist.

9. My children can always depend on me to provide for them.

10. I tend to give more advice than was asked for.

If you have six or more yes responses, you are probably a parent who criticizes and controls too much. If you have four yes responses and four sometimes responses, you have the tendency to be a parent who criticizes and controls too much. If you have five or more no responses, you are not a parent who criticizes and controls. Read on to determine which parenting style is yours.

Parents Who Defend and Deny

In each of the previous chapters we have investigated three of the four types of parents who misuse love to their children's detriment. If you have not identified with any of the first three types of parents, you may find you have something in common with the parent who defends and denies.

Of course you will not want to see anything in common with Donna (who was introduced in the first chapter, The Parent Trap) and her twenty-five-year-old son, Timmy, who is jobless, lazy, and living at home. Ironically Donna's heroic efforts at saving Timmy from the consequences of his behavior have left them both feeling like failures.

Donna: A Helicopter Parent

Donna was a protective mother who defended Timmy at all costs and denied his mistakes. Donna is a "helicopter parent," as outlined in Foster Cline and Jim Fay's book, *Parenting with Love and Logic*. According to Cline and Fay, overly protective, or helicopter parents, "hover over and rescue their children whenever trouble arises. They're forever running lunches and permissions slips and homework assignments to school; they're always pulling their children out of jams; not a day goes by when they're not protecting little junior from something—usually from a learning experience the child needs or deserves. As soon as their children send up an SOS flare, helicopter parents, who are hovering nearby, swoop in and shield the children from teachers, playmates, and other elements that appear hostile."

Donna took the helicopter concept a few steps further, from being an ineffectual parent by rescuing and defending, to being a parent whose love allows her to deny her son's problems. Timmy's problems, or Donna's denial of those problems, most likely caused Donna to divorce Timmy's step-father. Yet she says she got divorced because she did not want to be married to someone who did not like Timmy. One of the major differences between emotionally healthy families and emotionally unhealthy families is their recognition or denial of problems within the nuclear family.

Breaking the Denial Cycle and Recognizing Problems

In *No Single Thread*, researchers from the Timberlawn Psychiatric Hospital in Dallas found several consistent patterns that influence the emotional health of children within a family. One of those patterns was that emotionally healthy families identify problems within the family. Emotionally unhealthy families ignore and deny problems, such as alcoholism or severe depression, until the problem becomes so big or has caused so much damage that it cannot be denied. In the dysfunctional family, this behavior is often described as having an elephant in your living room that everybody walks around, but does not talk about. The children grow up with a family secret which inhibits their emotional development.

In contrast, the emotionally healthy family identifies problems and seeks professional help. The problem may not be totally solvable, as many problems are not, but these families improve their situation by making the best possible changes, and go on with their lives. Parents in healthy families have faith in the future together. They do not have blind faith or unrealistic dreams for the future; they just have an optimistic outlook punctuated with dashes of reality.

In Donna's family, Timmy was becoming the elephant in the living room. Her former husband had probably acknowledged this, and Timmy's older sister most likely complained about all of her mother's time and attention going to the elephant named Timmy. Unfortunately, after her complaints were discounted as sibling jealousy, Timmy's older sister may have believed her mother was right—she was simply not as loveable as Timmy.

Some teachers undoubtedly approached Donna with concern about Timmy's lack of effort, inability to take responsibility, and ability to manipulate people. As Donna denied the teachers' warnings, she probably convinced not only the teachers but also herself that Timmy did not have any serious problems. Both Donna *and* Timmy were in denial; any child wants to believe a parent who says "it isn't your fault."

Donna and Timmy were developing an emotionally un-healthy codependent relationship, based on Donna's need to be needed and Timmy's neediness. The vicious cycle was completed when his needs fed her neediness and her control-driven rescues rendered him emotionally crip-pled. Timmy had been raised never to take responsibility so Donna would have a secure role as his rescuer. To understand Donna and Timmy you must have a basic understanding of the concept of codependency.

Understanding Codependency

There are many lengthy definitions of codependency. One of the most brief is given by Melody Beattie in her book, *Codependent No More*. Here she describes a co-dependent person as one "who has let someone else's behavior affect him or her, and is obsessed with con-trolling other people's behavior."

In *Facing Codependence* Pia Mellody details five symp-toms with which codependents have difficulty:

1. Experiencing appropriate levels of self-esteem
2. Setting functional boundaries
3. Owning and expressing their own reality
4. Taking care of their adult needs and wants
5. Experiencing and expressing their reality moderately

In applying these five symptoms to Donna's story about her twenty-five-year-old son, Timmy, I think we can better understand both the concept of codependency and parents like Donna.

First of all, Donna could not have an appropriate level of self-esteem and allow Timmy to treat her the way she has. He does not help with the household chores or contribute financially to the maintenance of Donna's home. He disregards her basic rules by coming in at all hours, leaving beer cans and messy ashtrays around, leaving food out in the kitchen overnight, and leaving his clothes and junk all over the house. Moreover, Donna tolerates Timmy's disrespectful attitude and language, which is probably more abusive than disrespectful.

Donna has not established proper, enforceable boundaries. Pia Mellody explains boundaries as "invisible and symbolic fences that have three purposes: (1) to keep people from coming into our space and abusing us, (2) to keep us from going into the space of others and abusing them, and (3) to give each of us a way to embody our sense of 'who we are.'" Donna seems incapable of protecting herself from Timmy by setting and maintaining clear boundaries. She has created the elephant in her living room and now complains about his lifestyle.

Donna has a skewed sense of self. By this I mean that Donna's life and feelings have been influenced by what Timmy does or does not do. If you asked her who she is, she would probably begin by saying, "I'm Timmy's mother." Moreover, Donna would be at a loss if asked to continue describing who she is. Her identity has been defined by Timmy for so long that she probably has no sense of self. She is in a good mood if Timmy is in a good mood. When Timmy loses a job, it is her problem more than it is his. He does not need to worry or be depressed because she assumes the responsibility for him.

Like all adults, Donna has basic needs, such as food, shelter, and nurturing. A more specific need is respect. Donna thinks she deserves respect, but she does not know that she needs respect. Therefore, she does not insist on respectful behavior from Timmy. Disrespect from a family member, especially from an adult child, is emotional abuse. Donna does not provide any consequences when he disregards her rules or requests. Donna *wants* Timmy to respect her rules, but this is different from recognizing that she *needs* respect. Not being able to differentiate between a need and a want is a core symptom of codependency.

Last of all, Donna has great difficulty recognizing and confronting the reality of her son's behavior. Donna does not see Timmy as the manipulative and irresponsible young man that he is. She views Timmy as a good boy who has had a run of bad luck all his life. Codependent people usually see things as black or white. There is no grey for them. In reality Timmy has probably done some good things and some bad things. All of his failures cannot be blamed on others or on bad luck. Donna experiences Timmy's reality in extremes and therefore cannot see options but only one right answer. As Pia Mellody explains, codependents "are either totally involved or totally detached, totally happy or absolutely miserable." Donna has always been totally involved with Timmy, swinging from being totally happy to absolutely miserable.

Because Donna is a codependent parent, exhibiting each of the five core symptoms of codependency as described in *Facing Codependence*, she needs to seek therapy and join a twelve-step support group, such as Codependents Anonymous or Al-Anon. Only after Donna has an in-depth understanding of how codependence is destroying her life, will she be able to insist on Timmy contributing financially, physically, and emotionally to their family life. Recovery for Donna and other parents who defend and deny is possible through counseling and a twelve-step support group that requires consistent involvement and promotes growth.

Dana: Struggling with Denial

When Dana approached me for advice, I had a relatively brief conversation with her which led me to believe she and her husband Jeff were parents who alternated the role of defending their daughter, Jennifer, and denying her problems. At the time of her request for advice, Dana was trying to assess Jennifer's condition realistically, and Jeff was in a state of denial. Our conversation went something like this:

Dana began, "I need help. I am concerned about my fourteen-year-old daughter, Jennifer. I am worried about her eating habits and her low weight."

"Have you discussed this with her pediatrician?" I asked.

"Yes, and he says she's fine and we shouldn't worry because teenagers generally have poor eating habits."

"What does her father think?"

Dana replied, "My husband says I'm looking for trouble. He thinks I read too many magazine articles about anorexia. He jokes about me watching too many talk shows about eating disorders."

"Yet you are concerned enough to call me. It sounds like your motherly instincts are telling you Jennifer has a problem. Tell me more about Jennifer," I asked.

"Jennifer is a strikingly beautiful girl. She has two younger brothers who are thirteen and ten years old. She has always been so easy to raise because she has done everything right. She studies hard—maybe too hard. She had friends, maybe not one close friend, but she is always included in parties. Jennifer is a cheerleader and a good athlete. Her teachers say she is a model student. The last six months she has been busier than usual, yet she has always been able to work in time for jogging.

"I began to be aware that her clothes looked loose on her, more than just the oversized look. Then I noticed the small portions she would serve herself at dinner. She plays with her food by pushing it around on her plate. Maybe I am just comparing her to her brothers, who eat so much. However, when she carries her plate to the sink, she gives some excuse like she has to study or make a poster or something, and most of her food is still on her plate.

"Also I have watched her look at herself frequently in the mirror, looking to see if her stomach is flat. Her stomach looks more than flat to me; it looks concave. But she has this expression of disapproval, even disgust. Most of the time she seems about as happy as any fourteen-year-old. However, she also seems to be more distant or removed from the family. But isn't that also typical of teenagers?"

"Yes, teenagers do tend to try to separate from their parents, but there may be more going on here than typical teenage behavior," I suggested. "Dana, I must say my instinct is to trust your instinct. You sound like an intelligent, concerned mother who wants to be sure her daughter is well. You have checked with her pediatrician and discussed your concerns with your husband. Your description of Jennifer's behavior includes some alarming actions, especially the way she conducts herself at mealtimes and the way she analyzes her image in the mirror.

"I also hear you making a statement and then discounting what you have just said. Your husband may not be the only one who defends Jennifer's behavior and denies that she has a problem. I know you want to believe Jennifer is still your happy and normal child. Have you talked to Jennifer about your concern?"

"No, I haven't talked to her," Dana said, "I guess I don't know what to say. I am probably scared that I will say the wrong thing or that she won't tell me the truth. Then what would I do?"

"Maybe you are afraid she won't tell the truth or maybe you are more afraid that she will," I offered. "Part of denial is not being able to identify how you truly feel. Regardless, I recommend that you do not confront Jennifer with your fears yet, mainly because you and her father are not together on this issue. If Jennifer has an eating disorder, you and her father must both be willing to insist that she get professional help and be willing to go with her. It may be a long time before you and your husband are united on how Jennifer should be parented. Often when one parent takes on the role of the concerned parent, it frees the other parent to stay in denial.

"For the time being I strongly recommend that you go to counseling for yourself and by yourself. You have some emotional needs which are not being met. For example, your feelings of fear are being discounted; you deserve to be listened to. You have a right to be fearful and to be supported, whether the problem is an eating disorder or something else. Apparently your instincts and realistic perceptions are not being given the respect they deserve. You may have some childhood issues which were never addressed or resolved that cause you to doubt yourself and feel powerless as an adult.

"Eventually your whole family may need therapy. If Jennifer has an eating disorder, intensive family and individual therapy and participation in the twelve-step program, Overeaters Anonymous, can help Jennifer recover."

Dana: Six Years Later

Dana's next call came approximately six years later. After a quick review to remind me of who she was, Dana shared what her family had endured in the years following our consultation.

Dana recounted that she took my advice and went to counseling. Next she and her husband went for marriage counseling. Here Dana learned some coping skills and faced some major childhood issues which were inhibiting her emotionally. The counseling also helped her improve her relationship with Jennifer, who was rapidly sinking deeper into an eating disorder. Dana learned that she could not fix Jennifer. She learned that only Jennifer could decide to accept help for her disease. During the next five years Jennifer did a lot of lying, crying, and denying.

Dana was no longer in denial, but her husband Jeff was. The three had tried family counseling four different times, but Jennifer and her father stayed in denial. Not until the sixth year of Jennifer's disease did Dana and Jeff become

united in their fears for Jennifer and her eating disorder.
At that time they instigated a family intervention. Jennifer
was over eighteen, so they could not legally force her to go
for treatment. With each member of her family and a few
long-time friends confronting her in a professionally directed family intervention, Jennifer no longer denied her
disease and went into residential treatment.

Now Jennifer was completing college. Dana explained
that she would like to believe that Jennifer was in recovery and attending her support group meetings but she did
not know that to be a fact. Jennifer must be responsible
for her own recovery.

It is not a perfect ending. An eating disorder is a disease
of addiction. You do not get well, you can only get healthier. During all of the counseling Dana received, she became aware of her own addiction to codependency. She
takes care of herself and stays emotionally healthy by attending Al-Anon meetings.

Characteristics of Parents Who Defend and Deny

In the Broadway musical *Miss Siagon*, a mother sings a
song entitled "I Swear I'll Give My Life for You" to her
son. This could be the theme song for parents who give
and give in as well as for parents who defend and deny.
What these two types of parents have in common is that
their lives are so intertwined with their children's that it is
almost as if they had been absorbed by their children.
Ironically, in doing so, they have also taken their children's lives away from them. Obviously this is in extreme

cases. But it is the direction of consuming love that parents must be aware of.

Typically, parents who defend or deny have a positive outlook. These parents often see what they want to see. In more extreme cases, they live in a fantasy world, much like Donna, who saw her son Timmy as merely having a bad run of luck, and not as the irresponsible, narcissistic person he was.

Parents who defend and deny want peace and tranquility and think they can make it possible. They are good at comforting and listening to their children. They are not as good at listening to authorities or professionals—in these instances, they hear what they want to hear. They are always looking for ways they can manipulate people or situations to make the outcome wonderful.

These parents appear eager and enthusiastic to others. Their goals may be unrealistic, but their energy levels are so high that when they are in action, they can accomplish unbelievable tasks. Their enthusiasm can be catching and makes them fun to work with if you are not prone to be practical or analytical. If you are, their lack of logic and unrealistic ideas can drive you crazy.

Parents who defend and deny need recognition from their children. Just a word of thanks will keep them going for a long time. Timmy probably learned to manipulate his mother by using "please" and "thank you" at just the right time. If he ever said "I could not have done it without you," Timmy would have made his mother's year. Donna and parents like her thrive on recognition from those they love. Of course all parents like to be appreciated by their children, but no one enjoys it like a parent who defends and denies. The child's validation of his or her parent's worth serves as an affirmation that this child, whom the parent has been defending, is actually as wonderful as the parent has been claiming. Approval adds fuel to the fires of defense and denial.

Another characteristic for many of these parents is the tendency to do things in excess. It may be excessive eating or drinking, excessive shopping or giving. They often are impulsive when they make choices or decisions; they are rarely practical. They do not do things in moderation and often find themselves short of cash or with an unexpectedly high credit card bill. They act this way because it feels good at the time and seems to fill a need.

These parents will be seen at their children's schools, frequently volunteering and helping out in a multitude of ways. They love to interact with their children's teachers, coaches, and friends. This enables them to identify the fires they need to put out and to acquire connections so they can manipulate circumstances on their children's behalf. Being active and involved is also part of their codependency. Their lives are so intertwined with their children's lives that their happiness depends on their children's happiness.

Fears of Parents Who Defend and Deny

To understand why parents would express their love for their children by defending and denying, one must look at what these parents fear. Their greatest fear is rejection. Consider Donna: Her love for Timmy was so great that she defended him when he was wrong and denied that any of his mistakes were his fault. He was twenty-five, disrespectful, and dependent, and Donna would not stand up to him, much less kick him out of her home. She would never reject him because her greatest fear is that he would reject her.

Even Dana and Jeff feared rejection. They saw their place in the family as Jennifer's parents, who took care of the safety and health of their child. An eating disorder can be a fatal disease. If Dana confronted Jennifer with her fears, Jennifer might reject her. It took an even longer time for Jeff to face the truth. Dana felt that she would lose her place as the nurturing mother. Dana's codependency required her to try and control the harmful things in her child's life—even the things she could not control. The more she tried to control Jennifer's eating habits and weight, the further it drove Jennifer to exercise her control by limiting what she ate and what she weighed. Ultimately, both Dana and Jeff had to accept that Jennifer rejected their loving attempts at control.

In addition to fearing rejection, parents who defend and deny fear reality. At least that is what is most difficult for them to face. They are comfortable in the world they choose to see and believe. They have a role there. It may not be perfect, but they are familiar with it. Outside of their fantasy world and in reality, they fear they will have no role at all. They control the world as they know it and must stay in control at all costs. So reality is a foreign threat. For example, Donna did not want me to criticize Timmy because, in her world, she is the only one who can have negative thoughts about Timmy. She wanted encouragement to enforce her rules, but not advice about telling him to leave. Donna knows what to expect when Timmy uses and abuses her. She is very familiar with her chaotic life with him. But a peaceful life without Timmy is unimaginable.

What Parents Who Defend and Deny Can Do to Change

Parents who love too much by defending and denying can begin to make some positive changes in their lives by focusing more on themselves. When people seek counseling, they begin a process of examining and understanding their feelings. They are encouraged to focus on themselves and their childhood, family of origin, major life decisions, emotional needs, and much more. That is exactly what Dana did and she is taking care of her mental health now. She also is in the process of becoming the best parent she can be. It began when she called and said, "I need help." In so doing, Dana shifted her focus from Jennifer and her husband to herself. She started controlling the one person she could—herself. Dana is an exceptional example because she is making some great changes in her life and trusting her husband and Jennifer to take responsibility for themselves.

Obviously, parents who defend and deny need to work on thinking more logically. They must practice not trying to solve their children's problems or seeing themselves as the only ones who can make everything okay. This means rethinking their perceptions of reality. Dana's husband took six years to face reality. His daughter had an eating disorder that could kill her. Not until he could confront this reality himself could he confront Jennifer with it. His denial enabled Jennifer's denial. Likewise Donna's lying to herself enabled Timmy to lie to himself. Parents who live with a distorted reality teach their children to do the same.

Parents like Donna, Dana, and Jeff need to find someone to help them determine whether they are being objective, logical, and realistic in their perceptions. Perhaps a counselor or a trusted friend would be willing to verify their understanding or judgment of a situation. Members of a twelve-step support group are great at keeping each other tuned in to reality and on the track of logical thinking. Twelve-step programs also keep the focus on the self and not on others.

Last of all, parents who defend and deny must take responsibility for meeting their own needs. This process begins by identifying their basic needs. Parents who have difficulty taking care of their basic needs often do so because they have low self-esteem. In this case they should begin to surround themselves with the kind of friends who will help them build a stronger self-esteem. They should look for people to affirm their strengths and acknowledge their growth. Donna was seeking approval from Timmy. He had stopped expressing appreciation and started blaming her, along with everyone else, for his failures. Hopefully Donna will learn to give herself praise and recognition for her personal growth and develop friendships that will support her in making positive changes.

Another positive change for these parents would be to practice not saving their children from problems. For example, when Timmy was seven, he came to Donna with problems such as forgetting to do his homework. If she had refused to rescue him and cover up his mistakes, Timmy would have learned an invaluable lesson. He would have learned to take responsibility for his own actions, and not still be expecting his mother to solve his problems today.

Donna could have also taught Timmy to be responsible and independent whenever he came to her as a child with a problem by asking him, "What are some ways you have thought of handling this conflict?" instead of giving him her sage advice. When Timmy replied with a predictable "I don't know," she could have encouraged him to find a solution by saying, "You are such a smart boy, I'm sure you can think of something," then listening to him as he worked the problem out.

Undoubtedly Dana also missed some opportunities to give Jennifer the feeling of independence and self-control. For example, when Jennifer came to her mother, as all children do who want approval for what they do, and asked, "How do you like this picture (or project, poem, or performance)?" If Dana only replied, "I think it is great!" she missed an opportunity to teach the invaluable lesson of self-evaluation. If Dana had just added to her praise, "I want to know how you feel about it because you are the most important judge of your work," Dana would not have undermined her motherly authority, but she would have fostered in Jennifer the belief that even when no one else knows what Jennifer does, it is important for her to be proud of herself. This is a small but important step in teaching independence and responsibility. It can be frightening to those who see their parental role as being the chief defender of their children.

Could You Be an Overloving Parent Who Defends and Denies?

Read the following statements. The more openly and honestly you respond to each statement, the more you will learn—whether you are or could become a parent who defends and denies or another kind of parent who misuses love—about your parenting style. Respond with yes, no, or sometimes.

1. I try very hard to avoid problems.
2. I can see solutions to difficult situations.
3. I will lie to keep from getting into trouble.
4. I enjoy recognition.
5. I try to avoid conflict at all cost.
6. Critical people annoy me.
7. My life often feels overwhelming.
8. I love movies with happy endings.
9. My spouse says I'm impractical.
10. I like to escape into a good book.

If you have six or more yes responses, you are probably a parent who defends and denies too much. If you have four yes responses and four or more sometimes responses, you have the tendency to be a parent who defends and denies. If you have five or more no responses, you are not a parent who defends and denies. Review the previous types of parents to determine which parenting style is yours.

How to Make Loving
Your Child Work

Loving your child should be one of the most natural and wonderful parts of life. The maternal and paternal feelings for a newborn, innocent, helpless child are unlike any other kind of love. But as you have seen from the four types of parents who love their children in dysfunctional ways, just loving your child in a way that seems natural to you may not be the best thing for your child. Excessive love can backfire.

Whether you have identified with one of the four types of parenting styles or not, you want to be the best possible parent you can be. What follows are some suggestions for the most commonly asked parenting concerns, along with further resources.

Frequently I give lectures and make speeches at meetings and conferences. At the end of each presentation I generally invite the audience to ask parenting questions. After fielding parenting questions for more than fifteen years, I have discovered that parents everywhere have the same basic concerns and problems. Regardless of their race, religion, or socioeconomic status, parents always ask the same questions about sibling rivalry, discipline, self-esteem, bedtime, and chores.

I do not pretend to have the only answer to these problems because I believe that there is more than one way to solve a parenting problem, but I like parents to have "a bag of tricks" and as much information about parenting techniques as possible. I also trust a parent's instincts. If what I recommend does not feel right, I encourage him or her to tell me and ask for another idea or to get a second opinion from someone else.

I invite you to do the same. If my advice or approach to a parenting problem sounds like a good idea to you, try it. But remember, give yourself enough time to see if whatever you try will work. Initially any change or new approach, even if it is better, will be met with resistance because change is scary and threatening. Be sure to try it long enough so that everybody has a chance to see if they like the change.

Also, use consistently whatever parenting technique you choose. If you go back to your old ways, your child will not know what to expect and will not think you are in control. For example, if you set a rule that you will not drive your child to school if he misses the school bus and you give in after one week because he has a test that day, you have given your child the message that he can manipulate you into giving in, as long as he can come up with a good excuse, and your week of consistent parenting behavior is lost. Expect your rules to be tested and prove to your child that you mean what you say.

The Eight Most Important Parenting Challenges

Loving Unconditionally

To best understand unconditional love, it helps to look at the love most grandparents have for their grandchildren. Grandparents usually have an almost limitless capacity for loving their grandchildren. Grandparents do not base their self-worth on how successful their grandchildren are. Grandparents only want two things: good relationships with their grandchildren and healthy grandchildren. And grandparents usually get both. Often grandparents who were demanding and critical with their own children seem to have increased patience and understanding for their grandchildren. Their relationship brings joy, nurturing, and security to both grandparent and grandchild.

We also can learn about unconditional love from small children. Have you ever seen a toddler who did not love her mother because dinner was not good? She may push her plate away or refuse to eat the food, but that does not affect her love for her mother. Small children can be angry about something their parents have done and separate that anger from their deeper feelings of love for their parents. What a young child is capable of doing—separating the deed from the doer—many parents have great difficulty accomplishing.

Did a child ever stop loving his father because he did not attend his first open house at school? Did a grandparent ever withhold love from a grandchild for striking out in a baseball game? What children and grandparents have in common is their ability to love unconditionally. They love not for the way someone performs, appears, or succeeds. They love people because of who they are not what they are.

Do you express your love for your child when he disappoints you, embarrasses you, or disobeys you? These are the most difficult times to tell your child you love him, but they may be the most important times to reaffirm your love. Learn to separate your feelings for your child and your feelings about what he has done. An example would be to say, "I really don't like what you just did, but I still love you." Those words may feel awkward at first, but your child desperately needs to hear them. You may not feel your love for your child at the moment, but intellectually you know you love him. The feelings of love will return. Just expressing your love will facilitate the return of your affection.

Unconditional love is not easy for some parents to express because they did not receive it when they were growing up. Take a minute to reflect on how it would have felt to know that your parents loved you just because of who you were, not because of what you did? Well, it would feel just as wonderful to your child. Unconditional love will take practice. No one can make you feel love, but the good news is that expressing love is a learned skill. It is never too late to learn to say "I love you just the way you are."

Controlling Sibling Rivalry

Generation after generation of parents have complained about their children fighting. Typically parents describe their children as tattling on one another or picking fights. So many times I have heard, "Wherever I go or whatever I do, their fights follow me. I want them to be nice to each other. They don't have to love each other. I just want a peaceful home."

Sibling rivalry may be very common, but it does not have to be acceptable in your home. It is the parent's responsibility to make sibling rivalry unacceptable. The first step is to make stopping the fighting your number-one priority. Announce your intent to your children. Tell them in advance what the consequence for tattling or fighting will be.

Second, the parent needs to understand what is going on when brothers and sisters fight. Your children are seeking one thing—your attention. Each child wants you to love him or her more than you love your other child. There are two sure ways to recognize this tactic: your children follow you around the house with their fights, and their tattling or crying increases when you approach them.

Logically, if fighting draws your attention, then the fighting will continue. For children, it does not matter if your attention is good or bad as long as they get it. Parents often defend their tendency to give fighting children attention by explaining, "But I yell and scold them." Unfortunately, such a reaction is not helpful because the children have succeeded in getting the parent involved. That means they got your attention.

If you proceed to ask questions, give your opinion, or lecture, your children have won the battle by using sibling rivalry to secure your attention. Therefore, it is imperative that you withhold comments and involvement. Show no emotion. Enforce the consequences and go about your business.

What are appropriate consequences for fighting siblings once you have made a rule that fighting and tattling are no longer acceptable in your home? The consequences should be minimal for the first offenses of each day. I recommend sending the offenders to the dining room, or any boring room in your house. (You may send them to the same room, but sending them to separate rooms would be better if possible.) Say as few words as possible, such as "I see you have chosen to break the fighting rule. Go to the dining room."

An acceptable length of time in the dining room would be one minute for each year of your child's age. Following this rule of thumb, an eleven-year-old and an eight-year-old would be disciplined for about ten minutes. For each additional offense that day the time is increased by five minutes. Wipe the slate clean at the end of the day and start fresh each morning.

Use a kitchen timer. Set it for ten minutes and announce, "When you hear the beep, you may start playing again." When the beep sounds, say, "I feel sure you will remember that there is to be no fighting next time." Ignore complaints. Give no attention to either child, even the child whom you think might be the innocent one.

Your children will test you many times. Just when you think you have made believers out of them, they will test you again to see if they cannot get you to take sides and give them your attention. Now more than ever, you must enforce your consequence without becoming involved.

For additional support and information on sibling rivalry, read *Siblings Without Rivalry*, by Adele Faber and Elaine Mazlish.

Handling Problems at School

School problems worry parents because they fear that problems at school may lead to other troubles for their children. If a child's grades are not good, the parent worries how the child will get into college. If the child is a discipline problem, the parent worries about the child's reputation and future problems with the law. If the child is a bookworm, the parent worries about the child's social acceptance. If the child takes schoolwork too seriously, the parent worries about the child developing an ulcer. If the child is the class bully or the class victim, the parent worries that the behavior will continue into adulthood. You could probably add some of your own worries to the list.

Rarely are school days worry-free—and parents are right on target to take school problems seriously. With school dropout rates at an all-time high, and with the prevalence of teenage pregnancy, alcohol and drug abuse, and gang involvement, parents cannot help being concerned. But there are ways for parents of school-age children to avoid potential problems and to handle those that arise appropriately.

Become active and involved in your child's school. Attend PTA meetings, open houses, athletic events, and student performances. Initiate teacher conferences and be an advocate for your child. Volunteer your time to help in the school office, the classroom, the library, the lunch room or at a fund raising event.

Know what is expected of your child. Be familiar with the code of conduct, individual teacher's expectations, and grading systems. If you have a concern with something that happens in a classroom, begin by discussing it with the teacher. If the problem is not resolved, inform the teacher one more time of your feelings. If the situation still does not improve, inform the principal and seek her assistance. Following the appropriate chain of command will ensure the best resolution. Eventually your child should be encouraged to speak directly to his teacher about his problems.

Instill in your child the importance of receiving a great education. Share your dreams of a college education and a successful career of your child's choice. Match your words with your actions by showing interest in the papers your child brings home, the grades she makes, and subjects she takes. Read to your child and encourage her to read for pleasure on her own. Provide some structure at home by providing a place conducive to studying and by establishing regular mealtimes, study times, and bedtimes.

Homework is your child's responsibility, not yours. You have been to school and it is now your child's turn. Remember, your child's good grades are his reward. Your child will do better in school the sooner he feels that school belongs to him. He will have a sense of pride when he earns a good grade. When he turns in a project he has made, it may not be the best in the class, but he and his teacher will know he did it, not you.

If you receive a note or telephone call informing you that your child has been a discipline problem, thank the teacher for keeping you informed and encourage the teacher to enforce the usual consequences for the infraction. Express to your child your disappointment and disapproval for what she has done. Tell her you know she will not choose to make the same mistake again. In most cases, I do not recommend adding an additional consequence at home. Problems at school are best addressed and resolved at school. Frequently preschool teachers try to involve the parent in punishment for misbehavior at school. Be supportive of your child's teacher and express your confidence in his ability to handle the situation well.

What should you do if your child is an underachiever? Whenever grades are lower than a parent and teacher expect, my first thought is a learning difference, such as dyslexia, attention deficit disorder (ADD), or hyperactivity. Professional testing to determine if your child has a learning difference is essential. If a problem is identified in the tests, there are several methods of treatment that will improve your child's ability to learn. The better you are informed about your child's learning problems, the more helpful you will be in addressing them. There are two good books for parents in this situation: *Learning Differences*, by Donna Smith and John Turnbow, and *The Misunderstood Child*, by Larry Silver.

Once all learning differences have been ruled out, you can view your underachieving child as a discouraged learner. Others may feel she is lazy, disorganized, and uncaring. But I believe the underachiever is operating on a basic fear of failure. She would rather be considered lazy than dumb. Her belief is that it is better not to try and be labeled an underachiever, than it is to try and fail. Although tutoring often helps, nothing will make a tremendous difference until her self-esteem improves. Two helpful books for parents who have discouraged learners are *How to Help Your Child with Homework,* by Marguerite Radencich and Jeanne Shay Schumm, and *Why Is My Child Having Trouble at School?*, by Barbara Z. Novich and Maureen M. Arnold.

Promoting Good Self-esteem

Healthy self-esteem can make an average student a great student, will help a person have significant positive relationships, and will contribute to career success and happiness. No wonder parents want to know how they can give their children healthy self-esteem.

Self-esteem comes from children's perceptions of their relationships with the significant adults in their lives. The most significant persons in children's lives are their parental figures, followed by other close family, such as grandparents, then their teachers and their friends. If a child thinks his parents think he is smart, attractive, and a good child, he will develop good self-esteem. He decides what his parents think about him from the words they say and don't say, from expressions on their faces and the tone of their voices. Positive words like "I can always count on you," or disgust expressed in words like, "You have lost your homework *again,*" build or destroy self-esteem.

Parents should be aware of two major messages that build self-esteem. The first message is, "You are loveable." This message says, "You matter to me and I love you just because you are you. There is no one else like you. You are unique. My love is not earned. My love is unconditional and I will always love you."

The second message is, "You are worthwhile." This message says, "You can control your behavior and do the right thing. Moreover, you respect people and property. You have something to offer others, such as your teachers, friends, family, and those less fortunate. You may have feelings and opinions different from mine, which I will respect because you are worthy of respect. So if you are angry, I will not try to deny your feelings. If you do not like something I like, I will allow you to be different and I will appreciate your uniqueness."

Self-esteem can grow like a flower in a greenhouse. The perfect climate for cultivating a flourishing self-esteem is one in which trust is a main element. A home that has a trusting environment is a home where a child's needs are met. Beyond the basic needs of healthful food, appropriate clothing, medical care, and a clean place to live, a child has emotional needs. Emotional needs are met when a child is nurtured and allowed to express her true feelings (good or bad, happy or sad), to act like a child (age-appropriate, realistic expectations), and to be imperfect (everyone makes mistakes). A parent helps by saying things like:

- "I will tell you the truth."

- "I will be open with you and you can be open with me."

- "I will help you meet your needs."

- "I am not perfect and I do not expect you to be perfect either."

- "You are safe with me."

More specifically, to create a climate of trust, you must avoid unpleasant surprises, such as taking a child to the doctor without telling the child where you are taking him. Do not change the rules without explaining the change in advance. Avoid giving mixed messages, like saying you are not upset when your tone of voice and body language reveal your true, angry feelings. Mixed messages tell a child that he cannot trust what you say. A more trustworthy reply would be to admit your feelings and clarify that your angry feelings are not with your child but are caused by a problem at work or with whomever has made you angry.

I wish for you and your child a safe, loving home filled with people who encourage self-esteem. Remember it is easier to build self-esteem if you have self-esteem. But it is never too late to improve your self-esteem. Self-esteem is a learned concept, like expressing love, so work on changing yourself while you work on changing your child.

For more information on self-esteem I recommend reading *Your Child's Self-Esteem*, by Dorothy Corkille Briggs.

Establishing Realistic, Enforceable Rules

Rules give a child a sense of security. When a child knows what is expected and permitted, she has safe boundaries within which she can feel freedom and independence. However, I often talk to parents who try to enforce too many rules or rules that are too unrealistic. Let's look at the rules for making rules:

1. A rule must be reasonable for your child's age. A three-year-old should not be expected to make her bed every morning. A more reasonable rule for a three-year-old would be to put her toys back where they belong when she is finished playing with them. The parent of the three-year-old should expect his or her child to need friendly reminding and help in completing this task.

2. A rule must be understood by the child. A good way to test this criterion is to ask the child to repeat the rule and explain what it means to him. The child must know when he breaks a rule. If a rule is long, involved, and too detailed, chances are it is not likely to be understood or followed. Also the rule may be oversimplified

and destined to fail. A rule like "you must clean your room every Saturday" is an example of this. What "clean" means to your eight-year-old and what it means to you are two entirely different things.

3. The last rule for rules is that they must be enforceable. A rule is not good if it inspires a child to cheat or to break it because you are unlikely to know it has been broken. A rule such as, "Don't take a cookie from the cookie jar without my permission" is tempting your child to sneak a cookie because she knows it will be difficult for you to catch her. Do not make rules that require siblings to tattle on one another so that you will know if the rule has been broken. Such a rule only fosters sibling rivalry.

A few good rules are better than rules about everything. With a young child start with a rule about the right way to treat other people, such as, "Do not hurt others by doing such things as hitting, kicking, or biting." After the first rule is consistently obeyed, you can introduce another rule. Some rules will be learned and respected quickly, while other rules may take a month before children follow them every time. Some children obey rules the first time they are explained, and other children will test your limits constantly. The more consistently and unemotionally you enforce the rule, the more quickly the child will learn to obey it. But rules are not effective if there are not consequences for breaking them. Let's look next at consequences.

Implementing Consequences

Consequences are the prices you pay for making bad choices. For adults, a consequence could be getting a speeding ticket or being fired from a job. For children, a consequence could be getting a bad test grade or being grounded. The earlier a child learns that there are prices to be paid for making poor choices, the earlier the child will learn to be more responsible for his actions.

When your child breaks a rule or disobeys you, calmly say to your child, "I see you have chosen to (state the rule and the consequence)." In most cases the consequence for misbehavior is known in advance, so you will reiterate the expected consequence at the end of your statement. There is no need to scream or lecture. Give the impression that your child's choice to break the rule is not a problem for you, but it is a problem for her. Remember the importance of self-esteem. You must not expect perfection and must remember that everybody makes mistakes. You do not love your child any less, but there is a price your child must pay.

There are two types of consequences, natural and logical. I prefer natural consequences because they require nothing from the parent except that the parent allow them to occur. For example, a natural consequence would be if a child chooses not to eat a good breakfast, and then becomes hungry at school before it is lunchtime or if a child chooses not to study, and then does not get a good grade on a test. When a consequence occurs, a parent must not say, "I told you so." Parents may, however, ask, "Have you thought about how you will do things differently next time?" Parents must also accept their children's plans for improvement without criticizing or trying to improve them.

Logical consequences often require creativity and planning. With logical consequences, the goal is to make "the punishment fit the crime." I tell parents, "Don't drop the bomb on Luxembourg." By that I mean save big consequences for big offenses. If you overreact to little misdemeanors, then when your child makes a life-threatening mistake, you will have no convincing method of getting your child's attention and conveying that what she chose to do was awful.

Logical consequences are, whenever possible, related to the child's specific behavior. An example would be saying, "Because you misused a toy, you will not get to play with it for the rest of the day" (or longer if it is a second offense). With a teenager who speaks disrespectfully or hurtfully you would say, "Because you have chosen to speak to me that way, you are choosing to have no conversations with your friends on the telephone tonight."

Often "time-out," or time spent alone doing nothing in a designated place, is the most logical consequence. When a child's feelings surpass his ability to express those feelings in words, he may lash out physically. A few minutes in a "time-out chair" or being sent to another room is the best possible consequence. The child receives no attention for negative behavior and has time to regain his self-control. Parents can benefit from a time-out as well.

For more information on rules and consequences I recommend attending a focused parenting class at an agency such as the Parenting Guidance Center in Fort Worth, Texas. If you do not have parenting classes available to you, explore the resources at your church or synagogue or at your child's school. Often a school or church will provide parenting workshops if people request them.

Teaching Values

Many social problems have been blamed on the lack of values being taught in today's world. Parents must realize that they are the most important people in their children's lives and that they are the primary teachers of values for their children. Teaching values is being touted as the solution to many family and social problems. Children do need to develop a strong value and belief system and parents are the best at giving their children values. But values are better caught than taught. How can a child "catch" values? Just like catching the chicken pox, a child must be exposed to values to catch them.

A child learns values more from observing how her parents live their values than from listening to them talk about their values. Your child must not hear you say that you believe in honesty and then watch you do something that is not totally honest. If you allow this to occur, you undermine anything you have said about honesty. Children are at first confused about the difference between what parents say and what they do. Eventually they develop a set of values based primarily on how their parents behave. An example would be to tell your child not to drink and drive and then drive, with your child in the car, after you have had "just one glass of wine."

Another way a child develops values is through activities. Attending a church or synagogue regularly is a way for your child to learn more about your religious beliefs. Being involved in a scouting program or youth organization exposes a child to group morals and codes of conduct. Such involvement will also reinforce many of the values you have been teaching your child, such as respecting adults, protecting the environment, treating others the way they would like to be treated, and fair play.

Giving a child chores to do around the house and instilling a sense of pride in your child for a job well done, are ways of helping your child "catch" your values. Also give your child opportunities to earn money by doing extra jobs that are not a part of his regular chores. Encourage him to save part of the money he earns and allow him to decide how to spend the remainder.

Kids make great volunteers and learn values at the same time. They learn about helping those who are less fortunate. They also can experience how good it can feel to make a difference in someone else's life. Children can benefit from realizing that they can learn from the people they help. In doing so, they learn to value and respect people who are different from themselves.

As your child reaches adolescence, the values you have raised her with may conflict with her friends' values. As a concerned and loving parent, you will worry whether the values you have taught her will stick. Under peer pressure many adolescents succumb to the will of the group. In homes where children have been raised to judge themselves, to have a strong self-esteem, and to be self-disciplined, parents can be more confident that their children will resist peer pressure to go against their morals and values. Remember not to lecture your child, but to be encouraging by saying something like, "I trust you to make the right decision. I am here if you want to talk or just share your feelings." When your child can make moral decisions on his own, you deserve as much congratulations as your child. You haven't worked yourself out of a job yet, but your child is preparing for adulthood and you deserve much of the credit.

Encouraging Positive Behavior

Wouldn't it be great if your child wanted to please you all the time? Imagine not having to remind him to clean his room, to do his homework, to turn down his stereo, or to stop bugging his sister. It is unrealistic to hope that your child will never make mistakes, will always be responsible, and will be a perfect student. But it is not impossible to encourage positive behavior. As a matter of fact, positive behavior leads to more and more positive behavior, if the parent knows how to promote his or her child's desire to please and behave. The following are tried-and-true suggestions:

1. When your child does something good, let her know you have noticed and that you are proud, but be sure you do it in a way that will encourage her to repeat her good behavior. To do this, it is important to be specific about what you observed her doing. Telling your child she is the best girl places a great burden on her, because she knows she isn't perfect but suspects that you expect her to be perfect. Instead of saying, "You were the best girl today," which is a very general praise and doesn't identify specific behavior she will be able to repeat, say, "I noticed you let your friend play with your new toy— I think it is great when you share." When you formulate your praise after the second example, your child will understand exactly what behavior (sharing) you liked. This is achievable and repeatable. Moreover, your child does not feel guilty because she does not feel like "the *best* girl." Your daughter realizes that she can impress you by sharing. There is nothing a child wants to do more than to impress her parent. So your child will continue to share to make you proud. She will also feel loveable and

worthwhile, which, as you recall, are the feelings that
build self-esteem.

2. Do not focus your attention and praise on the end
results of your child's work. For example, when your
child brings home his report card, focus on his effort,
improvement, and time spent to make whatever grades he
earned—do not focus on the grade itself. Focusing on the
grade, the blue ribbon, or the score of a game says that
you value those things more than you value your child's
hard work and discipline.

Your child may not always be the winner or the best. If
you have communicated that the symbol of winning or
being the best is what you are proud of, then your praise
may backfire. An underachieving child will be discouraged and give up because he knows he will never get an A
grade. An overachieving child will not choose the most
demanding teacher because he fears he will not be able to
get As. Both children have misunderstood what you
value, which is the asset, the effort, the improvement, the
knowledge, and the experience. When the focus is placed
on these aspects, every child will feel successful.

3. All children want their parents' approval. From the
time they are very little, children seek their parents' opinions about everything they do. Even as adults, we still
want to impress our parents. However, when your child
comes to you with a picture he has drawn or a project he
has completed, and asks, "What do you think?" If your
answer is something like, "I like it. It looks great!," you
have missed an opportunity to encourage continued good
work.

All you need to add to your words of approval is the
question, "How do you like it?" This question tells your

child three things: First, it tells your child that you value his opinion. Second, it tells him that it is important for him to feel good about what he does. And third, it tells him that he is capable of judging his own work. Your child will still want your opinion and approval, but he will also begin to want to please himself.

Learning to be their own judge is an invaluable skill for children to have. Parents and teachers will not always be there to judge a child's work and behavior. What a comforting feeling it is for parents to know they have raised children who want to feel great about what they do, even when no one is looking. A child who has been raised to evaluate her own actions may make some life-saving decisions some day when she thinks, "My parents may never know, but I won't feel good about myself if I do this." Teaching your children to judge their own work and performance gives them the strength of character to do the right thing, even when no one knows.

4. Last of all, parents can encourage children to want to be contributing and helpful family members in the way they communicate "thank you." When your child does something to help you—whether it is an assigned chore or something in addition to what you expected—always say thank you. But sometimes do not stop with thanks. Occasionally slip in a few more meaningful words, such as "Thanks for clearing the table after dinner. Today was really hectic, and because you helped me, I could get out of the kitchen and relax sooner. I wonder if you know how much I value you and how glad I am to know you. You are an important part of the family, and I love you very much."

These are powerful words. Choose the words that feel right to you, but choose words that express need, appreciation, and love. Think about yourself and where you want to spend your time and share your talents. It is most likely a place where you feel loved, needed, and appreciated. If you have ever volunteered at a place where others did not tell you what a difference you made or how much you were appreciated, you probably did not continue to volunteer. Families are also like this and children are definitely like this. They will want to "hang out" in a family where they feel loved, needed, and appreciated. It is never too late to share those feelings with your children. When children know they are valued and important contributors to your family, they feel worthwhile. They will want to perpetuate that great feeling, and therefore they will continue to do the things that you appreciate and need.

Afterword

When I began this book, there were so many things I wanted to say to loving parents. It has been my job for the past sixteen years to respond to their concerns. But this book is different in that it gives me the opportunity of a lifetime to speak to loving parents whom I will never meet in person or through the media. It feels like a first chance as well as a last chance to make a difference for parents who really care.

I firmly believe, as many professionals in my field do, that the best way to help children is to help their parents. Being a parent today is more difficult than it has ever been. Likewise, growing up safe, happy, and healthy today is also more difficult than ever before.

So as I conclude this book, I do so with mixed feelings. I feel that there is so much more I want loving parents to think about. At the same time I feel hopeful that my ideas and suggestions will help parents with good intentions become the kind of parents they want to be.

If there were one more thought or suggestion I would want to share with parents who want a fresh start in their relationships with their children, it would be this: Make a list today of all the things you love and cherish in your child. Include things like "your smile" or "seeing you sleepy-eyed each morning" on the list. Tonight, invite your child to sit with you and privately read the list. Then tell your child that you know you make some mistakes every day, but that you are working on being the best parent you can be. Conclude with words of your choice, saying that you love and appreciate him or her and cannot imagine life without him or her.

I want to thank my own children, who have allowed me to almost work myself out of my job by being terrific young people. I could not have written this book if they had not taught me and loved me as much as they have. Each of them is uniquely wonderful. They have brought me laughter, excitement, joy, hope, and pride. I am always working on being the mother they deserve. I love each of them with all my heart.

Appendices

GUIDELINES FOR FINDING A COUNSELOR OR THERAPIST

• When looking for a family counselor, ask friends you respect and trust for references before going to other sources for recommendations. The Mental Health Association, your child's school counselor, your physician, or your minister or rabbi may also be able to refer you to a counselor.

• Before you begin any counseling, be sure the therapist is licensed or certified. Counselors operate under a number of titles, but the ones you are most likely to need will have the title of psychologist, guidance counselor, marriage counselor, or family therapist. All of these professionals should have a Master of Arts or Master of Science degree (M.A. or M.S.) or a Doctor of Philosophy degree (Ph.D) from a university that has an accredited psychology/mental health program.

• If you are considering going to a counselor or therapist, inquire about his or her specific area of training and expertise. Therapists are trained in many areas, but not every therapist is as skilled in working with particular age groups or types of problems. For example, some counselors are especially adept at working with parents who have teenagers, while others specialize in providing guidance for parents of younger children.

• Make an appointment for an interview with a therapist before you begin meeting with him or her on a regular basis. The interview session should take between fifteen and thirty minutes and you should expect to pay for this time. During the interview you should ask about the therapist's appointment cancellation policy and his or her approach to counseling families who have problems similar to yours. It also is acceptable to ask how long the average client works with him or her and to inquire about methods of payment. The interview also is your opportunity to ask about the therapist's specialized training, past experiences, and past successes.

• Be aware that you may not be able to develop a positive working relationship and rapport with a therapist who helped your best friend. If you feel uncomfortable with the therapist you have chosen, or think the counseling is not moving in the direction or at the speed you want it to, express your concerns and feelings to your therapist. If you do not agree with his or her response, or if you do not begin to feel better about your counseling, find another therapist. Remember you have a choice and the decision is yours—trust your instincts.

NATIONAL ORGANIZATIONS
FOR LOCAL REFERRALS

**American Association for Marriage and
Family Therapy**
1717 K Street NW
Suite 407
Washington, DC 20036
(202) 452-0109

American Association of Pastoral Counselors
9508A Lee Highway
Fairfax, Virginia 22031
(703) 385-6967

American Psychological Association
1200 Seventeenth Street NW
Washington, DC 20036
(202) 955-7600

Child Care Resources Clearinghouse
2116 Compus Drive SE
Rochester, Minnesota 55904
(507) 287-2220

Family Service Association of America
11700 W Lake Park Drive
Park Place
Milwaukee, Wisconsin 53224
1-800-221-3726

International Association of Biblical
Counselors, Inc.
P.O. Box 60730
Oklahoma City, Oklahoma 73105
(405) 843-7778

National Board for Certified Counselors,
American Association for Counseling and
Development, and American Mental Health
Counselors Association
5999 Stevenson Avenue
Alexandria, Virginia 22304
(703) 823-9800

United Way
701 N Fairfax Street
Alexandria, Virginia 22314
(703) 836-7100

Young Men's Christian Association (YMCA)
101 N Wacker Drive
Chicago, Illinois 60606
1-800-872-9622

Young Women's Christian Association (YWCA)
726 Broadway
New York, New York 10003
(212) 614-2700

ADDITIONAL RESOURCES
FOR PARENT SUPPORT
SERVICES AND INFORMATION

Parents as Teachers (PAT)
8001 Natural Bridge
Marillac Hall
University of Missouri
St. Louis, Missouri 63121
(312) 553-5738

An organization for first-time parents, intended to provide them with support from three months before a child's birth until the child is three years old. The organization's goal is to give new parents the confidence and knowledge to help them be better parents. Accessible through the public school system, PAT is free of charge for all parents.

Parenting Publications of America
12715 Path Finder Lane
San Antonio, Texas 78230
(512) 492-3886

An umbrella organization for parenting newspapers, newsletters, and magazines. Contact them at the above address to find the publications available in your area.

American Guidance Services
4201 Woodland Road
Circle Pines, Minnesota 55014
(612) 786-4343

Offers a practical and comprehensive course, called Systematic Training for Effective Parenting (STEP), for parents of children preschool age through middle-school age. It is offered by schools, community centers, health centers, churches, synagogues, adult education centers, civic groups, and counseling centers. The companion program, STEP/Teen, is also offered for parents of junior high and high school children.

SUGGESTED READING

Beattie, Melody. *Beyond Codependency: and Getting Better All the Time.* St. Louis: Harper and Row, 1989.

Briggs, Dorothy Corkille. *Your Child's Self-Esteem: The Key to His Life.* New York: Doubleday, 1975.

Chess, Stella and Alexander Thomas. *Know Your Child: An Authoritative Guide to Today's Parents.* New York: Basic Books, 1987.

Cline, Foster and Jim Fay. *Parenting with Love and Logic.* Colorado Springs, CO: Navpress, 1990.

Dinkmeyer, Don and Gary D. McKay. rev. ed. *Systematic Training for Effective Parenting Parent's Handbook.* Circle Pines, MN: American Guidance Services, Inc., 1989.

Elkind, David. *All Grown Up & No Place to Go: Teenagers in Crisis.* New York: Addison-Wesley, 1984.

Elkind, David. *A Sympathetic Understanding of the Child: Birth to Sixteen.* Boston: Allyn, 1978.

Elkind, David. *The Hurried Child: Growing Up Too Fast.* New York: Addison-Wesley, 1989.

Lewis, Jerry M., Robert Beavers, John Gossett, and Virginia A. Phillips. *No Single Thread.* New York: Brunner/Mazel, 1976.

Mellody, Pia. *Facing Codependence: What It Is, Where It Comes From, How It Sabotages Our Lives.* San Francisco: Harper, 1989.

Novick, Barbara Z. and Maureen M. Arnold. *Why Is My Child Having Trouble at School?* New York: Villard, 1991.

Radencich, Marguerite and Jeanne Shay Schumm. *How to Help Your Child with Homework: Every Caring Parent's Guide to Encouraging Good Study Habits & Ending Homework Wars.* Minneapolis: Free Spirit, 1988.

Rydman, Edward. *Finding the Right Counselor for You*. Dallas: Taylor, 1989.

Silver, Larry B. *The Misunderstood Child: A Guide for Parents of Learning Disabled Children*. New York: McGraw Hill, 1988.

Zink, Jay. *The Zink Method*. Gardina, CA: Iwate, 1981.

Notes

Notes

Notes

Notes

Notes

Notes

Notes

Notes

ABOUT THE AUTHOR

Beverly Browning Runyon, a native of Fort Worth, Texas, and a graduate of Vanderbilt University, chaired the task force that developed the Parenting Guidance Center in Fort Worth and served as its founding president. She is currently the Director of Community Relations for the Center.

For nine years she has appeared weekly on the local NBC affiliate's noon news to offer parenting advice. She is also seen regularly on the nationally syndicated call-in television show *Cope*. A parenting and family consultant for more than fifteen years, she is also a partner in the training and consulting firm Training Unlimited.

She and her husband, Bill, a pediatric dentist, have six children. They live in Fort Worth, Texas.